The Methadone Briefing

An easy to use reference guide to methadone and methadone prescribing: for health and other professionals

**The Methadone Briefing was
written and edited by:**
Andrew Preston, RGN, RMN, Community Nurse,
Drug Team, West Dorset Community Alcohol and
Drugs Advisory Service, Dorchester.

Contributing authors:
Gerald Bennett, BSc, MPhil, PhD, AFBPs, SCPsycol,
East Dorset Drug Team.
Sile O'Connor, BSc (Pharm), DAS, MPSI, MRPhS,
Addictions Directorate Pharmacist, Maudsley
Hospital, London.
Philip Fleming, FRCPsych, Consultant Psychiatrist,
Portsmouth Health Care NHS Trust, Northern Road
Clinic, Portsmouth.
Mike Blank, RMN, General Manager, Derwen NHS
Trust, Carmarthen.
Francis Keaney, MB, MICGP, Registrar in Psychiatry,
The Maudsley Hospital, London.
John Derricott, RGN, RMN, Drug Trainer, HIT,
Liverpool.
Tom Aldridge, BA, MPhil, CQSW, Freelance Trainer
and Consultant.
Janie Sheridan, Phd, MRpharmS, Research
Pharmacist, The National Addiction Centre, London.

ISBN 0 9520600 19

Published by Andrew Preston, 1996.

Design: Andrew Haig & Associates/Roger Harmar.

Printed in the UK by Island Press.

Distributed by: ISDD, Waterbridge House,
32-36 Loman Street, London SE1 0EE.

Peer reviewers:

Michael Farrell, National Addiction Centre.
Mary Glover, MSc, BSc, CQSW, Social Worker, CADAS drug team, Dorchester.
Kim Hager, Director, Exeter Drugs Project.
Andy Malinowski, BA, MSc, CQSW, Director, Druglink, Swindon.
John Merrill, Consultant in drug dependence, Drugs North West, Manchester.
Duncan Rastrick, MRCPsych, Mphil, Clinical Director, Leeds Addiction Unit.
Harry Shapiro, Institute for the Study of Drug Dependence, London.
Nick Wilson, RGN, RMN, Project Manager, CADAS, Dorchester.

We are grateful to Martindale Pharmaceuticals for an educational grant which has made this publication possible.

Your comments and suggestions for future editions of *The Methadone Briefing* will be gratefully received. Please send them to:
Andrew Preston
c/o CADAS, 28 High West Street,
Dorchester, Dorset DT1 1UP.

Thanks also to the following for their help in checking facts and offering advice and suggestions for the book:

Jackie Ackhurst, Medical Information, Britannia Pharmaceuticals.
David Beattie, Senior Translator/Medical Writer, Hoechst Rousell Pharmaceuticals, UK.
John Davies, Wellcome Foundation.
Driver and Vehicle Licensing Authority, Swansea.
Pam Fields, Wigan CDT.
Alan Fisher, Martindale Pharmaceuticals.
John Gerrard, Home Office Drugs Inspectorate.
Russ Hayton, Plymouth Community Drug Service.
Hoechst AG, Germany.
Debbie Preston.
Andy Rose.
Martin Shepard, Dorset County Hospital Drug Information Service.
T Snewin, Pharmacist, Law Department, Royal Pharmaceutical Society.
David Taylor, Clinical Director, Pharmacy Department, Maudsley Hospital.
Andrea Ward, Senior Medical Information Officer, Hoechst Rousell Pharmaceuticals, UK.
The Wellcome Trust Library.
Simon Wills, Drug Information Service, Portsmouth Hospital.

Special thanks to:

The peer reviewers (listed above) for all their suggestions and advice.
John Witton and Annie Ryan at the ISDD library and information service for their work in finding dozens of articles and references, often at short notice.
Christine Compton for proof reading and compiling the peer review draft.
Janet Whitehouse for proof reading the final draft.
Karin Woodruff for compiling the index.
Tom Aldridge for his invaluable advice and help as Project Consultant.

And finally:

Hello to Todd, Sam and Rachel.

contents

Foreword   **6**

Section   **1** The history of methadone
                      and methadone prescribing   **7**

Section   **2** The research basis for
                      methadone prescribing   **23**

Section   **3** Methadone manufacture and
                      the preparations available   **31**

Section   **4** Physiology and
                      pharmacology of methadone **39**

Section   **5** Methadone and the law   **65**

Section   **6** Assessment   **75**

Section   **7** Treatment aims and
                      treatment choices   **89**

Section   **8** Getting the starting
                      dose right   **105**

Section   **9** Methadone detoxification   **115**

Section 10 Practical issues in
                      methadone prescribing   **129**

Section 11 Prescribing for groups
                      with special needs   **141**

References   **151**

Index   **157**

foreword
by Dr Michael Farrell

Methadone prescribing remains a highly controversial and contentious activity. Despite reasonable evidence of its benefits there remains a deep suspicion and antipathy among drug users, drug services, professionals and the broader community to methadone and other substitute prescribing.

The generality of this negative attitude makes the long-term viability of such services uncertain and very vulnerable to hostile criticism. Much of the discussion and criticism are based on belief systems, be these treatment, religious or philosophical. Some such criticism may not be amenable to change in the light of empirical evidence on the effectiveness of substitute treatment.

This book provides a comprehensive background on the history, research, pharmacology and legal aspects of methadone prescribing. It focuses on this single substance in practical aspects of assessment, treatment aims, dosages and detoxification and should be a valuable reference for workers in the field.

In looking at substitute prescribing there are three dimensions of consideration:
1. The type of drug prescribed and its properties, the administration system which includes whether the drug is taken on or off site and whether it is consumed with or without supervision
2. What other sorts of rules and contingencies are associated with the administration of the drug, and
3. The types of psycho-social interventions associated with the first two, including vocational training, education, counselling, psychotherapy, physical health care, and welfare and legal rights information.

It is clear that methadone prescribing can be well done or badly done, and badly delivered methadone treatment may be substantially worse than badly delivered treatments that do not involve prescribing. The principle of 'do no harm' needs to be carefully observed in the context of substitute prescribing.

Andrew Preston has performed a monumental and scholarly task in pulling all this information together.

The section on the history of methadone should put some well worn myths to rest: in particular the text points out that the name 'Dolophine' – which was reputed to be derived from Adolf Hitler – was not in fact created as a trade name until after the war, by the Eli-Lilly pharmaceutical company, and was probably derived from the French words 'dolor' (pain) and 'fin' (end).

Finally as the area of substitute prescribing becomes more textured, issues such as the balance between short-term maintenance and long-term maintenance and oral and injectable prescribing is well argued and will provide the basis for further discussion on these subjects.

I am certain that this text will be a valuable guide for those embarking on the challenging but rewarding task of working with drug users to help them achieve greater control over their lives.

section 1

The history of methadone and methadone prescribing

The origin of legal controls	8
The Rolleston report	8
The discovery of methadone	9
The 1960s	13
The 1970s	14
The 1980s	15
The American experience	16
Prescribing services available in the UK today	18
Key events in the history of prescribing	20
Summary	22

Introduction

Responses to opiate use vary across the world and are, in many ways, as much a product of history as of anything else.

Understanding the history of responses to opiate use puts into context the prescribing policies we see today – and may help us anticipate the future.

Starting with the first organised responses to opiate use in the UK this section describes the influences on policy and practice, including those from the USA, the history of the discovery of methadone and the development of its unique role in the treatment of opiate use.

The services offering a treatment response to opiate use that are currently available in the UK are then described in the light of the historical background.

The origin of legal controls

At the turn of the century most countries had few laws restricting the possession of drugs.

Growing international concern about opiate use led to the First Opium Convention in the Hague in 1912. Britain as a signatory agreed to the principle of adopting controls over opium, morphine and cocaine.[1]

In July 1916, following rumours that soldiers on leave were using cocaine, a 'Defence of the Realm Regulation' was enacted making it illegal to possess cocaine unless prescribed by a doctor.

In 1920 and 1923 the list of drugs that were illegal to possess, import or sell was expanded by the Dangerous Drugs Acts to include opium and opium derivatives such as heroin. Doctors could still prescribe these drugs, but each prescription could only be for a maximum of three collections from the pharmacy.

This caused some concern among doctors because it left them unclear as to when prescribing these drugs was legitimate and was seen as Home Office interference with medical autonomy.

In 1924 the Ministry of Health set up a committee, chaired by Sir Humphrey Rolleston, to look into these issues.

The Rolleston report

This report, published in 1926, accepted the principle that all doctors could legitimately prescribe addictive drugs as part of the treatment of dependence.

The report argued that abstinence should be the long-term goal of treatment, but also accepted that long-term prescribing was a legitimate way of treating people who were unable to stop taking drugs.

It recommended that two groups receive treatment with morphine or heroin, namely:
**a) Those who are undergoing treatment for the cure of addiction by the gradual withdrawal method, and
b) Persons for whom, after every effort has been made for the cure of the addiction, the drug cannot be withdrawn either because:**
> **(i) complete withdrawal produces such serious symptoms which cannot be satisfactorily treated under the normal conditions of private practice; or
> (ii) the patient, while capable of leading a normal life so long as he takes a certain non-progressive quantity, usually small, of the drug of addiction, ceases to be able to do so when the regular allowance is withdrawn.**

This pragmatic approach in which the care of opiate users was entrusted to doctors continued without serious review until the late 1950s. However the number of people being treated at any time was only a few hundred – and they were generally considered to be stable.

When the first statistics were compiled in 1935 they counted 700 'addicts'. About one sixth of these were medical practitioners. This size and pattern of addiction remained similar through the 1930s, '40s and '50s. In 1959 there were 454 known addicts of whom the majority (204) were addicted to morphine, 68 to heroin and 60 to methadone. 76% had become addicted following treatment for pain and 15% were health professionals.[2]

The discovery of methadone

The origins of the research

In 1939 Otto Eisleb and a colleague O Schaumann, scientists working for the large chemicals conglomerate I G Farbenindustrie at Hoechst-Am-Main, Germany, discovered an effective opioid analgesic drug which they numbered compound 8909 and called Dolantin.[3] This was the discovery of pethidine. As with diamorphine (heroin) before, and buprenorphine (Temgesic) since, the early hopes of it being 'a new non-addictive analgesic' were not realised.

However the powerful analgesic action of pethidine was much needed during the Second World War. It was being produced commercially by 1939[3] and at the height of the war in 1944 annual production had risen to 1600 kg.[4]

Meanwhile close colleagues Max Bockmühl and Gustav Ehrhart were working on compounds with a similar structure to Dolantin in the hope of finding:
■ Water-soluble hypnotic (sleep-inducing) substances[5]
■ Effective drugs to slow the gastrointestinal tract to make surgery easier[6]
■ Effective analgesics that were structurally dissimilar to morphine – in the hope that they would be non-addictive[5] and escape the strict controls on opiates.

There is no evidence, as had been widely believed both here and in the USA, that they were working as part of a German attempt, directed by Hitler, to replace opium supplies which had been cut off by the war.

This myth has been widely expanded to attributing one of methadone's first trade names – Dolophine – to being a derivation of Adolf and even that it was called Adolophine in Germany – the 'A' being dropped after the war. In fact the name Dolophine was created for the drug as a trade name after the war by the Eli-Lilly pharmaceutical company in America. It was probably derived from the French dolor (pain) and fin (end).[6]

The discovery of 'Hoechst 10820': methadone

During 1937 and the spring and summer of 1938 Bockmühl and Ehrhart worked on the creation of another new substance in the group which they called 'Hoechst 10820' and, later, polamidon.

A patent application was filed on 11 September 1941 and the discovery was formally credited to Bockmühl and Ehrhart (see overleaf).[7]

It has been asserted that because the new compound's two-dimensional structure had no resemblance to morphine its pain-killing properties were not recognised until after the war had ended.[6] But although the town of Hoechst was extensively bombed during the war the I G Farbenindustrie factory suffered only slight damage and so limited experimental work was able to continue, stopping only when supplies of coal ran out or when the rail links were broken. In the autumn of 1942, after it had been determined that the drug was both an analgesic and a spasmolytic, it was handed over to the military for further testing under the code name Amidon.[8] There was no attempt to try and get polamidon production levels up to those of pethidine. Construction continued at Hoechst on a new pethidine production plant.[4]

DEUTSCHES REICH

AUSGEGEBEN AM
25. SEPTEMBER 1941

REICHSPATENTAMT

PATENTSCHRIFT

№ 711069

KLASSE **12p** GRUPPE 1 01

I 62426 IV d 12 p

✳ **Dr. Max Bockmühl und Dr. Gustav Ehrhart in Frankfurt, Main-Höchst** ✳

sind als Erfinder genannt worden.

I. G. Farbenindustrie Akt.-Ges. in Frankfurt, Main

Verfahren zur Darstellung von basischen Estern

Patentiert im Deutschen Reich vom 15. September 1938 an

Patenterteilung bekanntgemacht am 21. August 1941

Gemäß § 2 Abs. 1 der Verordnung vom 20. Juli 1940 ist die Erklärung abgegeben worden,
daß sich der Schutz auf das Protektorat Böhmen und Mähren erstrecken soll.

Gegenstand des Patents 710 227 ist ein Verfahren zur Darstellung von basischen Estern durch Umsetzung von Diarylessigsäurenitrilen mit basisch substituierten Halogenalkylen und Überführung der erhaltenen tertiären Nitrile in die zugehörigen Ester.

Es wurde nun gefunden, daß man zu diesen basischen Estern auch dadurch gelangen kann, daß man Metallverbindungen der allgemeinen Formel

$$R_1 \atop R_2 \Big\rangle C \cdot CO_2R \atop Me$$

worin R_1 und R_2 Arylreste, die auch unter sich gebunden sein können, Me ein Alkalimetall und R einen Alkyl- oder Aralkylrest bedeuten, mit basisch substituierten Halogenalkylen, wie z. B. Piperidinoäthylchlorid, Diäthylaminoäthylchlorid, Morpholinoäthylchlorid u. dgl. umsetzt. Man stellt zweckmäßig zunächst die Natriumverbindung des Diarylessigsäureesters her, z. B. durch Einwirkung von Diäthylacetonitrilnatrium u. dgl. auf den Diarylessigsäureester, wobei gleichzeitig Diäthylacetonitril zurückgebildet wird. Auf die Natriumverbindung des Diarylessigesters läßt man dann ein basisch substituiertes Halogenalkyl einwirken. Man kann aber auch z. B. die Kaliumverbindung des Fluoren-9-carbonsäureäthylesters durch Einwirkung von Kaliumalkoholat auf Fluorencarbonsäureäthylester darstellen und damit das basisch substituierte Halogenalkyl einwirken lassen. Die neuen Verbindungen sind hervorragende Spasmolytica und Analgetica.

Beispiele

1. Zu 4,6 g Natriumdraht, der mit 50 ccm Benzol überschichtet ist, läßt man unter Rühren eine Mischung von 9,7 g Diäthylacetonitril und 11,2 g Chlorbenzol eintropfen. Die Temperatur wird durch Kühlen zweckmäßig

An explanation for it not being exploited more fully between 1939 and 1945 was given by Dr K K Chen – an American doctor who did much of the early clinical research work after the war – who said a former employee of I G Farbenindustrie had told him in personal correspondence that they had discounted its use because of the side effects.[8] Chen presumed that the doses used in the experiments had been too high, causing nausea, overdose etc.

After the war

All German patents and trade names, including those for polamidon, were requisitioned by the allies as spoils of war. The I G Farbenindustrie factory was in a US occupation zone and therefore came under American management. The US Foreign Economic Management Department sent a 'Technical Industrial Intelligence Committee' team of 4 men (Kleiderer, Rice, Conquest and Williams) to investigate the war-time work at Hoechst.

In 1945 The Kleiderer report was published by the US Department of Commerce Intelligence. For the first time in print it reported the findings of Bockmühl and Ehrhart; and that despite having a different structure, polamidon closely mimicked the pharmacological action of morphine.[9]

The formula was distributed around the world and exploited by many companies, which is why it has so many different trade names. As a result this production of analgesics, which was no longer commercially viable, practically stopped at Hoechst after the war. The pethidine plant, by then half finished, was instead dedicated to the production of penicillin.[4] The I G Farbenindustrie empire was broken up by the allies and the plant that had developed methadone became part of a new company called Hoechst A G.

Eli-Lilly and other American and UK pharmaceutical companies quickly began clinical trials and commercial production of the new drug, polamidon.

In 1947 Isbell *et al,* who had been experimenting extensively with methadone, published a review of their experimental work with humans and animals and clinical work with medical patients.[10] They gave volunteers up to 200mg 4 times daily, and found rapidly developing tolerance and euphoria. They had to reduce levels with patients on these high doses because of, among other things: '…signs of toxicity…inflammation of the skin…deep narcosis and…a general clinical appearance of illness.' They also found that 'morphine addicts responded very positively.' They concluded that methadone had high addiction potential:
'We believe that unless the manufacture and use of methadon [methadone] are controlled addiction to it will become a serious health problem.'

There were many early studies all of which found methadone to be an effective analgesic. Bockmühl and Ehrhart were not able to submit the preliminary research results that they had given to Kleiderer on the 60 or so compounds they had discovered in the 'new class of spasmolytic and analgesic compounds' until July 1948. They were published in 1949.[11]

An early advert for physeptone

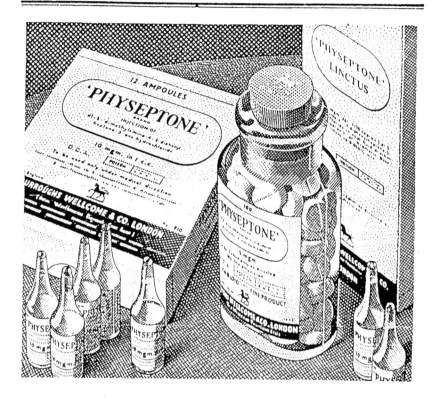

LII   THE PRACTITIONER

For control of severe pain

Clarity of mind; absence of constipation; little risk of addiction; and an analgesic effect superior to morphine — these features have established 'Physeptone' as the drug of choice for the relief of severe pain in patients confined to bed. Compressed products of 5 mgm., in bottles of 25, 100 and 500. Injection, 10 mgm. in 1 c.c., in boxes of 12.

For control of cough

The cough-suppressive action of 'Physeptone' is comparable with that of diamorphine but without the attendant risk of addiction. Since the effective dose is considerably less than that required for analgesia, it is best prescribed as 'Physeptone' Cough Linctus, a pleasantly-flavoured preparation containing 2 mgm. in each teaspoonful. Packs of 2 fl. oz. and 20 fl. oz.

'PHYSEPTONE'
Amidone Hydrochloride

'PHYSEPTONE'
LINCTUS

BURROUGHS WELLCOME & CO. (The Wellcome Foundation Ltd.) LONDON

Early use in the UK

The earliest accounts of methadone use in the UK were from papers published in the *Lancet* in 1947 describing it as 'at least as powerful as morphine, and 10 times more powerful than pethidine' and, subsequently, a study of its use as an obstetric analgesic at the University College, London.[12] This study, however, was terminated because of respiratory depression in the newborn babies.

Early advertisements claimed that Physeptone (Wellcome's trade name for methadone) carried 'little risk of addiction' and the consensus was that it was a better analgesic than morphine. It is therefore likely that the first people who became dependent on it had either been treated for pain or treated by doctors who thought it to be less dependency-forming than other opiates.

In 1955 the Home Office was aware of 21 methadone addicts; by 1960 the number had risen to 60.[2] In 1968 when the present Home Office notification system was set up the first two notifications arrived on 1 January: a 19 year-old female from London SW12 and a 20 year-old male from London SE23. By the end of the year 297 people had been notified as addicted to methadone.[13] In 1969, as a result of the setting up of clinics (see below) the number of people reported as using methadone had risen to 1687.[14]

The 1960s

In 1958, at the instigation of the Home Office, the Department of Health set up a Committee on Drug Addiction to review policy in the light of the new synthetic opiates that had come on to the market. The report, often called the 'First Brain Report', was published in 1961. Its conclusions were, effectively, an endorsement of the Rolleston report.

In the early 1960s the number of opiate addicts increased and the pattern of use began to change: there were younger people and more people taking opiates for pleasure rather than as part of medical treatment.

Heroin first overtook morphine as the most notified drug of addiction in 1962.[15] Most of these 'new' addicts lived in London. All of the heroin was pharmaceutically pure and much of it was prescribed by a small number of doctors.

There was concern that, contrary to the principles of the Rolleston report, some doctors were showing little, if any, inclination to 'make every effort for the cure of addiction'. This concern led to the recall of the Committee on Drug Addiction in 1964.

The second Brain report

This report was published in 1965 and resulted in changes in policy and the law:
■ The right to prescribe heroin and other specified controlled drugs for the treatment of addiction was restricted to doctors licensed by the Home Office
■ Doctors were legally required to notify addicts to the new Home Office Addicts Index
■ Drug clinics were set up to provide specialised medical treatment of addiction.

Contrary to the belief of many doctors methadone has never been one of the controlled drugs that can only be prescribed by specially licensed doctors.

The late 1960s

By 1966 there were 6 times more notified heroin addicts than morphine addicts.[15]

In 1968 the new drug clinics began operating. Their establishment attracted a large population of opiate users into contact with the service and the number of notified addicts rose to 2881 of whom 2240 were addicted to heroin. The clinics were set up to:
- Provide a legal supply of drugs
- Attract heroin users into contact with the service
- Prevent the illicit market in drugs
- Prevent the crime associated with illicit drug use
- Help people get off drugs altogether.

In the first years of the drug clinics they prescribed drugs that the clients were already taking, mostly in injectable form. Some clinics had 'fixing rooms' where injecting equipment was provided so that clients could inject their medication.

By the end of 1969, in central London, diverted supplies of injectable methadone, mostly in the form of Physeptone ampoules and 10mg diamorphine tablets, were huge. These tablets were known as 'Jacks' which is the origin of the phrase 'Jacking up'. Indeed Physeptone ampoules were so easily available on the black market that they were used:
- As a suitable sterile fluid to flush out and clean injecting equipment between 'hits' of 10mg diamorphine tablets
- Instead of water to dissolve drugs
- As a 'freebie' to encourage bulk sales of the 10mg diamorphine tablets.

These supplies came from both the clinics and a small number of doctors in central London who had large numbers of opiate users on their lists to whom they prescribed freely.

The 1970s

During the 1970s the incidence of heroin use continued to rise. For the first time this included a significant quantity of imported, illicit heroin.

The clinics started to doubt the efficacy of prescribing the client's drug of choice as a way of producing change. Clinic prescribing practice moved away from predominantly prescribing injectable heroin towards prescribing oral methadone, on the basis that it was more therapeutic to prescribe a non-injectable drug and because its long half-life meant it could be taken once daily rather than every few hours.

A landmark study from that time (and the only randomised controlled trial in this area) compared the effects of randomly allocating heroin users to either of these two treatments.[16] The study, carried out by Martin Mitcheson and Richard Hartnoll between 1971 and 1976, found that methadone treatment produced more polarised effects than heroin treatment. The methadone group were more likely to leave treatment but were also more likely to achieve abstinence. The heroin group were more likely to stay as they were. The researchers concluded that:
'The provision of heroin maintenance may be seen as maintaining the status quo, although ameliorating the problems of acquiring drugs ... by contrast the refusal to prescribe heroin (and offer oral methadone instead) may be seen as a more active policy of confrontation that is associated with greater change.'

As the results of this study became available the clinics were starting to deal with a new and different client group: large numbers of working-class heroin users who were smoking rather than injecting the relatively cheap heroin that had appeared on the market from the Middle East.

In the light of the changing client group – who were not asking for injectable drugs – and the results of the study, the clinics defined their role as one of promoting change and increasingly moved towards the use of oral methadone.

The shift away from maintenance prescribing

Some clinics began to review the efficacy of maintenance prescribing. For example a small study carried out in 1975 by the Glasgow Drug Clinic found that ceasing to prescribe methadone to new patients led to them improving as much as maintained patients, except in the area of crime.[17] Although weak scientifically, the publication of studies such as this in the late 1970s led to questioning of the value of maintenance prescribing, or, indeed, any prescribing.

The 1980s

In the early 1980s there was a second period of dramatic increase in the prevalence of heroin use. The numbers of notified addicts which had increased slowly through the 1970s from 509 in 1973 to 607 in 1976 and to 1110 in 1979, doubled from 1979 to 1982 and had doubled again by 1984.[18]

This great increase in the early 1980s differed from that of 20 years earlier, in that it was not restricted to London: it occurred all over Britain and many of these new users smoked their heroin (known as 'chasing the dragon') rather than injecting it.

The prescribing response was largely one of methadone mixture detoxification programmes – the 'gradual withdrawal method' of the Rolleston report.

However the increase in the number of opiate users meant that services had to expand and become more widely available. Prompted by this change and the Advisory Council on the Misuse of Drugs (ACMD) Report on Treatment and Rehabilitation[19] the Government responded with a funding initiative which saw the development of a non-statutory drug service and/or a Community Drug Team in most health districts. Most of these new services got involved in methadone prescribing either by employing a clinical assistant or a consultant psychiatrist on a sessional basis to prescribe methadone, or through working with GPs.

AIDS and the re-emergence of maintenance prescribing

The possibility of rapid transmission of the HIV virus among intravenous drug users and reports of high HIV prevalence figures among intravenous drug users in Edinburgh prompted a fundamental review of drugs policy.

The 1988 report of the Advisory Council on the Misuse of Drugs (ACMD) on AIDS and drug misuse[20] Part 1 led to the development of community-based needle and syringe exchange schemes all over Britain.

The report articulated the policy of directing treatment towards abstinence by achieving intermediate goals such as:
■ Stopping injecting with unsterile equipment
■ Taking drugs by mouth or inhalation
■ Taking prescribed rather than illegal drugs.

The report advocated a comprehensive approach to the prevention of the spread of HIV, following its first conclusion that:
'**...HIV is a greater threat to public and individual health than drug misuse. The first goal of work with drug misusers must therefore be to prevent them acquiring or transmitting the virus. In some cases this will be achieved through abstinence. In others, abstinence will not be achievable for the time being and efforts will have to focus on risk reduction. Abstinence remains the ultimate goal but efforts to bring it about in individual cases must not jeopardise any reduction in HIV risk behaviour which has already been achieved.**'

This reversed the abstinence-orientated prescribing policy of the preceding years as it legitimised longer-term prescribing to enable users to stop injecting. Although there was a wider range of prescribing options supplementing short-term detoxification, most doctors continued to prescribe methadone mixture only for limited periods of time.

In time it transpired that the high HIV infection rates in Edinburgh were a local phenomenon resulting from factors such as unavailability of injecting equipment, and were not being replicated across Britain.[21, 22] However the services that were set up on the assumption that these HIV prevalence rates were typical have almost certainly been instrumental in maintaining relatively low rates of HIV seroprevelance among injecting drug users.

The opposition to methadone maintenance prescribing

This shift was not universal. The prescribing clinic in Sheffield was disbanded and replaced by short-term in-patient detoxification and residential rehabilitation.[23] At first in Edinburgh – where the epidemic of HIV had left half of the city's injectors HIV positive – methadone was only offered to those who were HIV positive. It took until 1988 to establish a co-ordinated prescribing service.[24]

In Merseyside some doctors revived the prescribing of heroin in injectable and smokeable forms.

The 1980s conflict over prescribing policy led many to regard as a *cause célèbre* the disciplining of Dr Anne Dally who had espoused maintenance prescribing. The General Medical Council found Dr Dally guilty of 'serious professional misconduct' because she had 'irresponsibly treated addicts privately by providing methadone in the long term without reasonable medical care.' Some saw this as punishment by the medical establishment for her policy of maintenance prescribing and prescribing of injectables as part of private practice.[25, 26]

The American experience

It is helpful to understand the American experience with methadone maintenance because:

- This is where the concept originated
- Of the different ways in which treatment has been delivered there
- Much of the research into methadone treatment has been carried out in the USA.

The American experience shows that treating patients with the same medication can be viewed and executed in very different ways, and that these may be as important as the drug itself in determining the effects of treatment.

From the First World War onwards American and British drug policies took very different directions. In the USA in 1914 the Harrison Act controlled the sale and possession of drugs. It contained references to the prescription of addictive drugs for 'legitimate medical purposes...prescribed in good faith'. However in 1922 the Behrman case, in stark contrast to UK policy, determined that it was a crime for a physician to prescribe a narcotic drug to an addict.

By 1938 approximately 25000 doctors had been prosecuted on narcotics charges and 3000 had served prison sentences! Federal agents relied heavily on the testimony of drug users to secure these convictions – they secured these testimonies by supplying the users with small quantities of drugs.[6] Understandably this resulted in doctors having very little to do with the treatment of addiction.

After the Second World War there were just two large drug treatment facilities providing in-patient treatment to 'help addicts abandon drug taking'. The one at Fort Worth in Texas offered a service to men who lived west of the Mississippi and the one in Lexington in Kentucky served men east of the Mississippi and women from the entire USA.

The first use of methadone in the treatment of opiate dependence

An account of the first use of methadone in the treatment of addiction given by Dr M J Kreek in 1989 is quoted by Thomas Payte.[6]

In the early 1960s Dr Marie Nyswander and Dr Vincent Dole, a respected American psychiatrist and research scientist, had found that they could not stabilise opiate users on morphine without continually increasing the dose. They reviewed the medical literature in search of possible alternatives and pioneered the radical step of prescribing methadone which was effective orally, and seemed from pain research and some detoxification experience to be longer acting (they were not able to measure blood levels in those days). They soon found that once they had reached an adequate treatment dose that they could maintain people on that dose for long periods of time.

Dole encountered powerful resistance from the US Bureau of Narcotics whose agents told him that he was breaking the law and that they would 'put him out of business'. In view of the past history of doctors' experiences in court he took the brave step of inviting them to prosecute so that a 'proper ruling on the matter could be made' – they declined.

Nyswander and Dole: the pioneers of American methadone maintenance

Within a year Nyswander and Dole had developed 'Methadone Maintenance Treatment'. Their experiments with this approach began with treating people in a locked ward with elaborate security procedures. The project soon discovered that this level of security was unnecessary and it was gradually abandoned by moving first to an open ward, and then having patients reside in the ward whilst they went out in the daytime to work. This innovative treatment was offered only to people with a long history of heroin use and failed treatment.

Nyswander and Dole based their approach on the theory that, once addicted, opiate addicts suffer from a metabolic disorder, similar in principle to metabolic disorders such as diabetes. Just as insulin normalises the dysfunction in diabetes, so methadone was proposed to normalise the dysfunction of opiate addiction. They argued the necessity for large doses of methadone (80mg to 150mg) to establish a 'pharmacological blockade' against the effects of heroin, that would prevent addicts from experiencing euphoria if they took it.

Even though Nyswander and Dole viewed methadone treatment as a physical treatment for a physiological disorder, their initial attempts to use methadone maintenance were combined with intensive psycho-social rehabilitation. Many of their patients clearly derived great benefit from this innovative treatment.[27]

The spread of methadone maintenance programmes

This new form of treatment spread rapidly in the USA but was often implemented in a rigid way that lost some of the characteristics of Nyswander and Dole's original work. Consequently few programmes have produced such good results as their early work. The ways in which it was implemented in the early 1970s were strongly affected by political and other factors, with extensive government regulation.

The medical treatment was – and is – encased in a rigid delivery system. In most programmes patients attend the programme daily to drink their methadone and are regularly monitored through testing of urine samples (the collection of which is supervised) and counselling. Some programmes offer a variety of help and psycho-social treatment from group therapy to help in finding jobs. Once patients are stabilised they are able to earn the 'privilege' of taking home doses of methadone for one or more days.

The numbers of patients receiving Methadone Maintenance Treatment (MMT) in the USA rose: in 1992 there were about 120 000 patients served by around 800 programmes.

There is a great deal of variation in the rehabilitation and psycho-social services that are offered in addition to methadone and also in the dosage levels employed. Over half of patients receive below 60mg daily – which is accepted in the USA as the therapeutic minimum[28] – well below the level recommended by Nyswander and Dole's research.

Prescribing services available in the UK today

Methadone prescribing services in the UK could be described as a patchwork, with most areas having a service of some kind but with many variations between health districts. The titles of services can vary a lot but, in addition to GPs, there are three main types of community service:
- Street agencies
- Community drug teams
- Drug clinics.

There are also a small number of doctors who offer treatment to drug users as part of:
- Private medical practice.

General Practitioners (GPs)

Everyone has the right to have a GP. Although many refuse to treat drug dependency all GPs are entitled to prescribe methadone (and most other drugs) in order to treat addiction. GPs notify nearly half of all those treated with methadone.

They do not usually have in-house testing facilities such as urinalysis, but primary health care teams increasingly have staff such as counsellors in their surgery.

GPs vary considerably in their attitudes and practice in treating drug problems. If a GP is not inclined to prescribe methadone for an opiate user there is little that can be done to force them because doctors are able to use considerable discretion in deciding what they think is the best treatment for their patients.

Street agencies: easy-reach, often non-statutory services

Such services are often called the 'Drug Advisory Service' or similar and tend to be based in town centres, designed to be easily accessible and easy to approach. They may be staffed by a mix of paid staff and voluntary workers, usually providing a telephone helpline, advice and counselling, needle exchange and guidance on how to access residential rehabilitation and detoxification or methadone treatment. They usually serve a wide range of people with drug problems, and their families.

Community drug teams (CDT)

Statutory services are usually staffed by nurses and social workers and in some cases also by clinical psychologists, probation officers, counsellors, and/or medical practitioners. Some community drug teams play the same role as street agencies, but usually focus on a prescribing and counselling service. They may have their own doctor to prescribe, or may liaise with the patient's GP to put together a package of care involving monitoring and counselling from the CDT. CDTs tend to serve mainly opiate users, but usually have a remit to help people and their relatives with other types of drug problems.

Drug clinics

Drug clinics tend to be based in hospital and emphasise out-patient medical care; they are often headed by a consultant psychiatrist, but staffed by doctors, nurses, social workers, and possibly occupational therapists and/or clinical psychologists.

Clients may have to attend on a daily basis or several times a week to obtain their prescriptions. In some cases, usually 'low threshold methadone maintenance programmes', they may be required to drink their methadone at the clinic in front of a member of staff.

To cope with the large volume of prescription writing most clinics use a computer to generate prescriptions – see Section 5: methadone and the law, handwriting exemptions. These prescriptions may then be sent to retail pharmacies for dispensing. Alternatively, methadone may be dispensed from a local hospital pharmacy as this is often cheaper.

Drug clinics may have access to specialist in-patient facilities for detoxification and other in-patient treatments. Some clinics have facilities for dispensing methadone to patients who have to attend daily to receive their medication. Drug clinics usually offer a variety of treatment options.

Large centre prescribing is often an essential part of a service to a large number of opiate users, hence their predominance in large cities.

Private practice

Despite the experience of Dr Anne Dally (see above) there are still a small number of doctors in private practice who prescribe oral or injectable methadone to drug users. Some do it out of a belief in the need for more sympathetic, responsive services and offer a useful adjunct to the NHS. Others are not so principled, and some of these are still a source of drugs for the illicit market, and are of little therapeutic value to their patients. However, large dose, unsupervised prescribing is not confined to private practice and is a feature of a minority of all service types.

In general, private services are preferred by clients who are in full-time employment, and appreciate the shorter waiting times, increased doses and willingness to prescribe on a maintenance basis.

Key events in the history of prescribing

Note: To give an indication of the growth of opiate use column 2 in the following table shows the annual numbers of addicts known to the Home Office expressed as multiples of the 616 that were known in 1936.

Year	Relative number of addicts 1936=1	Total number of addicts	British events	Events outside UK
1869			UK Pharmacy Act restricts the outlets for sale of opiates	
1914				USA: Harrison Act restricts drug supply
1916			Defence of the Realm Regulation restricts drugs	
1920			Dangerous Drugs Act	
1922				USA: Prescription of addictive drugs illegal
1923			Dangerous Drugs Act	
1926			Rolleston Report: addiction a medical matter	
1936	1.0	616		
1942	0.8	524		Germany: Hoechst 10820 – later to be named methadone – discovered
1945	0.6	367		USA: commercial production of methadone begins
1958	0.7	442	First 'Brain' Committee set up	
1961	0.8	470	First Brain Report restates Rolleston approach	
1963	1.0	635		USA: Nyswander and Dole pioneer Methadone Maintenance Treatment (MMT)
1964	1.2	753	Second 'Brain' Committee set up	

Year				
1965	1.5	937	Brain Report recommends changes to law, prescribing, and Addicts Index	
1968	4.7	2881	Drug clinics set up	
1970			Clinics begin shift to oral methadone	USA: methadone maintenance spreads
1975	5.6	3425	Shift away from maintenance prescribing	
1980	8.3	5107		
1983	16.6	10235	First drug injector dies of AIDS	
1985	23.8	14688	Central Funding Initiative funds expansion of drug services	
1988			ACMD report on Drugs and AIDS expansion of harm reduction	
1990	28.8	17755		
1993	45.4	27976	ACMD follow-up report AIDS and Drugs Misuse endorses methadone maintenance	
1994			Drug Treatment Effectiveness Review commissioned	

summary

■ British policy has always been a pragmatic mix of harm reduction, abstinence, and social control.

■ Prescribing policy has clearly never been a purely medical issue, although it responded to medical advances, such as the development of methadone.

■ It is impossible to separate health responses from legal and political responses.

■ Talk of 'prescribing policy' and 'the British System' can give the false impression of a monolithic, uniform treatment system – this is far from the truth.

■ People who wish to advocate change often seize on research findings (whether valid or not) or a specific sentence from a report to buttress their arguments for change in an unbalanced way.

■ Debate about prescribing policy has oscillated between polarised viewpoints.

■ Most doctors change their practice more slowly than the researchers and policy makers advise.

■ Methadone was not invented as part of a German war effort to replace supplies of opium and Dolophine was an early American trade name: not a derivation of Adolf.

section 2

The research

basis for

methadone

prescribing

Research methods   **24**

Research findings on methadone
detoxification   **26**

Research findings on methadone
maintenance   **27**

Summary   **30**

Introduction

The research into methadone in the management of opiate use has looked extensively into its uses for detoxification and maintenance.

Methadone has been used for both treatments because it:
- Is cross-tolerant with most opiates, and so can be substituted for them
- Can be taken orally, helping drug takers to move away from injecting
- Is long acting, and therefore needs to be taken only once a day as opposed to the more frequent administrations required by drugs such as heroin.

Care must be taken in drawing lessons from studies carried out in one place and applying them to services in another. In particular it must be remembered that much of the work on methadone maintenance has been carried out in the USA where :
- Patients receive their medication in a very different way to patients in the UK
- Street heroin has been less pure than in Europe
- Cocaine use has been much more prevalent than in Europe.

It is also important to bear in mind the prevailing drug and treatment trends of the time as this can have an influence on the outcomes of a study.

There are different types of research which measure different things in various ways. The methods of research that have been carried out are outlined below, followed by the findings.

Research methods

Randomised controlled trials
The most conclusive method of answering questions about the effectiveness of any treatment is to do a randomised controlled trial in which patients are randomly allocated to different treatments so that differences in outcome can be attributed to differences in treatments.

There have been only a small number of randomised controlled trials in the study of methadone maintenance and detoxification.

The only British randomised controlled trial of maintenance, comparing maintenance treatment using either methadone mixture or heroin was carried out in the early 1970s when heroin maintenance was the norm. They found that heroin maintenance kept more patients in treatment, but caused less change in them than did methadone. This might not be found now, 20 years on, in a different culture where methadone mixture is the norm and offering it is less confrontational.

Social and economic factors have also dramatically changed since then, as evidenced by the authors' comment that: **'...addicts were rarely unemployed for external reasons ... when patients wished, they had little difficulty in obtaining work or training'.**[16]

The value of work for people abandoning opiate use and the associated lifestyle demonstrates the need for judgement in generalising the research from one time and place to that carried out in another.

Descriptive studies
Descriptive studies are interesting and valuable, but their findings cannot establish cause and effect because there is no 'control group' with which to compare the changes in the study group. For example, an American study in 1991 of 633 patients receiving methadone maintenance found that patients on higher doses of methadone were less likely to take heroin.[29] From this alone one could not conclude with certainty that higher dosages of methadone caused patients to take less heroin: there are other possible explanations.

Relationship beween methadone dose and heroin use: Adapted from Ball and Ross, 1991.

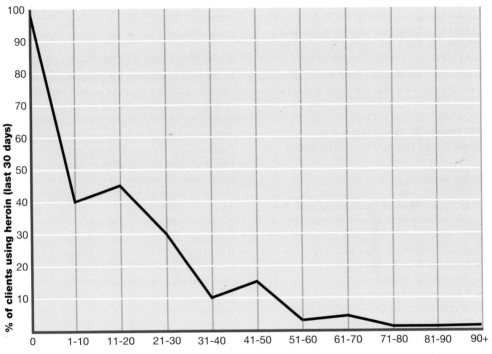

Descriptive studies such as this are helpful and thought provoking and can suggest questions that can only be answered by experimental studies. In this instance a subsequent double-blind randomised controlled trial which compared 0mg, 20mg and 50mg of methadone daily, found that larger doses were more effective in suppressing heroin use.[30, 31] The suggestion that came from descriptive studies was confirmed by a randomised trial.

Descriptive studies are sometimes the only practical way of studying some topics. For example Hubbard et al carried out a very large study of 11 750 drug users who entered treatment for drug dependence in 1 of 41 American programmes between 1979 and 1981.[32] The study followed them up for three to five years after terminating treatment, in order to compare the outcomes of those receiving three very different treatments:

- Methadone maintenance
- Drug-free residential programmes
- Non-prescribing out-patient programmes.

It would be almost impossible, although invaluable, to carry out such a study as a randomised trial. Nevertheless the results are extremely interesting and suggest further questions to be answered.

The most interesting observations were that in the long run each type of treatment produced very similar results, despite their very different approaches, and that the best predictor of outcome in any of these three approaches was the time spent in treatment. The time spent in treatment was more important than the type of treatment.

Perhaps treatments work by giving people the opportunity (albeit in very different ways) to modify their behaviour whilst in treatment, and the longer the opportunity to abandon old behaviour and develop new patterns of behaving, the more likely it is that these will persist after treatment and unlock further change. So although this study lacked the tight control of a randomised trial to disentangle cause and effect, it provided valuable and thought-provoking findings.

Research findings on methadone detoxification

Isbell and Voge[33] published an account of methadone's use in detoxification in 1948. They concluded that it was much safer than many methods of detoxification used since 1900, which included treatments which had significant mortality rates such as:
- Belladonna sleep treatment
- Bromide sleep treatment
- Insulin sleep treatment
- Sodium thiocyanate – which triggered psychotic states in some patients.

A review carried out in 1938[34] had concluded that most treatments were either useless or dangerous or both, and that the best approach was a 10 day gradually-reducing treatment of morphine and codeine. Methadone seemed much safer than all of these.

Much of the British research on methadone detoxification has been carried out on its use with in-patients.

Subjective experience of withdrawal symptoms
In a series of studies at the Bethlem Royal Hospital in Kent, Michael Gossop and colleagues have examined patients' responses to methadone detoxification.[35]

A study of the effects of a 21-day withdrawal regime on patients' withdrawal symptoms[36] found that the intensity of withdrawal symptoms started rising after the 10th day of treatment, and reached a peak on the 20th day, the last day on which patients took methadone. Withdrawal symptoms then started to subside, but it took another 20 days for them to reach a low level. This means that newly detoxified patients are very vulnerable for some time.

A further study showed that the intensity of withdrawal symptoms was determined not by the amount of opiates the person had been taking, but by their level of anxiety.[37] Many studies of patients' reactions to unpleasant medical procedures had found that a major cause of anxiety was patients' unclear expectations about what they would experience. The study also found that removing uncertainty, by teaching patients about what they were likely to experience, caused them to be less anxious.

Green and Gossop[38] carried out an experiment in which a total of 30 patients were detoxified as usual, but 15 of these patients were also taught in detail about the pattern of symptoms that they were likely to experience over time. Those who received education experienced milder withdrawal symptoms than the others, and were also more likely to complete treatment.

10 and 21 day detoxifications
A further study[39] compared completing methadone withdrawal over two periods – 10 days or 21 days. A similar pattern of withdrawal symptoms occurred in each group except that withdrawal symptoms peaked on the 13th day in the shorter treatment, compared with the 20th day in the longer treatment.

Although those receiving the 10 day treatment experienced more intense withdrawal symptoms, just as many (70%) completed detoxification.

Short term detoxification using methadone and heroin

Gossop and Strang[40] compared the responses of heroin users and methadone users to a 10 day methadone detoxification treatment. The methadone users experienced more severe withdrawal, especially during the first 10 days (when they took methadone). They experienced much more intense insomnia, muscular tension, weakness, and aches and pains. However despite more painful withdrawal, the methadone users were just as successful as heroin addicts in completing treatment.

Methadone detoxification with out-patients

Considering most detoxes in Britain are carried out in the community there is very little UK research into methadone detoxification with out-patients.

Two treatment trials carried out by the Maudsley Community Drug Team suggest that short-term detoxification is not, in terms of achieving sustained abstinence, very effective.[41, 42] A randomised controlled trial comparing out-patient and in-patient detoxification found that only 17% of out-patients and 81% of in-patients completed treatment.

A further study compared two out-patient methadone detoxification programmes. One group of patients were given a fixed dose reduction schedule over 6 weeks. The other group were able to negotiate their rate of reduction, with the aim of reducing to nothing in about 6 weeks.

Those receiving the fixed reduction were three times as likely as the others to complete detoxification. For all patients 40% of urine samples taken during the detox contained evidence of other opiates, but only 28% of patients completed treatment.

Although this sort of out-patient detoxification may not be effective in terms of achieving lasting abstinence it can be a useful tool in helping the client understand the nature of

their drug dependence. This can be maximised if clients are carefully assessed and offered support and counselling during and after the detoxification.

Research findings on methadone maintenance

Randomised controlled studies

A study in Bangkok[43] compared a 45-day period of methadone maintenance with a 45-day methadone withdrawal. The withdrawal group were 6 times more likely to drop out of treatment than the maintenance group and were 10 times more likely to have an opiate positive urine test result.

A New York study in 1991[29] compared the effects of methadone alone versus no medication for people on the waiting list for a comprehensive maintenance programme. The methadone group were three times more successful in stopping taking heroin during this period and twice as likely to start on the comprehensive programme at the end of the waiting list.

These studies demonstrate the value of methadone maintenance, even without additional counselling.

Three randomised controlled trials, one each in the USA[44], Hong Kong[45] and Sweden[46], compared methadone maintenance with a no-treatment control group. The trial in each country was carried out soon after the treatment became available there. This meant that the people in the no-treatment control group would not have had access to methadone maintenance so preventing the ethical problem that arises when people are denied treatment that has been shown to be effective.

Each trial used people who:
■ Were current opiate users
■ Had at least a 4 year history of opiate use
■ Had relapsed after at least one previous episode of rehabilitation.

The US study compared methadone maintenance with a no-treatment waiting list and found that at the end of a year the control patients were 97 times more likely to be using heroin daily than the treated group, and 53 times more likely to be in prison.

The Hong Kong study compared methadone maintenance with maintenance prescribing of a placebo medication, under double blind conditions. In this study the placebo group were started on methadone and then had their methadone gradually replaced by a placebo under double blind conditions. All patients received intensive counselling and support, but by the end of three years the placebo group were 63 times more likely to have been discharged from treatment because they had returned to heroin use.

The Swedish study compared methadone maintenance plus vocational rehabilitation with a no-treatment control and found that at the end of two years the treatment group were 38 times more likely to have stopped regular illicit drug use.

These three studies show that methadone maintenance is more effective than no treatment in reducing illicit drug use with its attendant health risks and criminal activity.

Treatment duration and change
In 1989 Hubbard et al carried out a national study of drug treatment effectiveness in the USA.[32] They found that the longer people stay in treatment (beyond a minimum of 3 months) the better they do in the long term.

This may reflect self selection of the more motivated patients for longer treatments, or it may show that each treatment is effective and that the longer patients receive it, the more lasting the improvements they make.

Dose level and behaviour change
Nyswander and Dole's pioneering studies used large doses of at least 80mg of methadone daily to establish 'pharmacological blockade'. The theory being that if enough methadone is taken it blocks all of the opiate receptors so that taking heroin in addition would have no effect.

Subsequent implementation of methadone maintenance in the USA often used lower doses. Descriptive studies have repeatedly found larger doses to be associated with less heroin use and the US National Institute on Drug Abuse (NIDA) recommended 60mg of methadone as a minimum effective dose.[30]

British prescribing has typically used lower doses, with the rationale of giving just enough methadone to abolish withdrawal symptoms, without increasing the level of dependence, or causing other harm, such as accidental overdose or inadvertently feeding the illicit market.

Whether or not Nyswander and Dole's hypothesis about the protection of 'pharmacological blockade' is true in Britain is open to question. Street heroin in Britain has tended to be much purer than in the USA and it may, therefore, be more potent in overcoming any 'pharmacological blockade'.

In 1993 Strain and colleagues reported a double blind trial comparing the effects over 20 weeks of medication containing 0mg, 20mg, or 50mg methadone daily.[30,31] The larger the dose the more people stayed in treatment and the more they reduced their heroin use. This shows that methadone dosage does have a real effect on outcome and raises the possibility that doses greater than 50mg would have achieved greater improvements.

Using treatment incentives to help reduce other drug use
A significant problem for methadone prescribing has been that some patients who stop using heroin continue to use non-prescribed drugs such as benzodiazepines and alcohol.

One method of reducing additional drug taking has been to systematically link incentives with reductions in illicit drug use and increased stability. Examples of incentives intrinsic to methadone treatment are the frequency of dispensing from a pharmacist (in the UK) or of 'take-home' doses (in the USA).

In one randomised treatment trial[47] half the patients who took additional drugs were given take-home doses of methadone after achieving heroin-free urine samples: the other half received the same number of take-home doses, but on a random basis. Of those receiving the doses linked to improvements, a third improved: hardly any of the others did.

Reducing the use of drugs such as benzodiazepines may well improve peoples' mental state and allow them to make further improvements in functioning. The systematic use of incentives is a cheap, safe way of reducing additional drug use by patients on methadone.

Methadone maintenance programmes: descriptive studies

Studies have tried to examine the differences between programmes to identify whether some are more effective than others. Clearly some are more effective but these studies can suggest, but not prove, factors that may underlie the differences.

A landmark study by Ball and Ross[48] looked in detail at 6 methadone programmes and carried out independent assessments of 633 male patients and repeated it on 507 of these patients a year later. They found an overall improvement in patients, but great differences between programmes. For example overall 71% of the patients had stopped injecting drugs but the rates for this in individual programmes varied from 43% to 90%.

Better outcomes came from programmes with better counselling services and an orientation toward maintenance and rehabilitation. Higher doses of methadone were associated with lower levels of heroin use.

These findings suggest, but cannot prove, that psychosocial treatment and methadone dosage are very important; they have been followed up by randomised trials, described above.

Counselling and psychosocial interventions and change

Programmes which offer more of such facilities tend to get better results. Nyswander and Dole's original treatments involved intensive rehabilitative efforts. A trial which compared three levels of psycho-social treatments coupled to methadone maintenance found that more intensive help and counselling led to better results.[49] Just 'policing' methadone by urine testing and interviews was inadequate. Adding counselling virtually halved the numbers of urine samples that contained illicit opiates. Adding additional psychological and social services resulted in further reductions in illicit drug use as measured by urine screening, and also brought improvements in:

- Alcohol use
- Employment
- Criminal activity
- Mental health.

Since all patients received the same methadone programme, these differences are entirely due to the differences in psycho-social services. Compared with the patients in the counselling condition of this study, British patients maintained on methadone usually receive a rather low level of counselling and support.

Treatment programmes which accept that opiate dependence is a chronic condition, and that methadone treatment is required as long-term stabilisation, tend to produce greater change than those which see it as a short-term treatment leading to abstinence. Also counselling that is compulsory and not client centred is unlikely to be helpful and may even be counter productive.

summary

■ Studies are embedded in their social and historical context, and this always needs to be considered.

■ As with many other pharmacological treatments, there is much more to methadone treatment than methadone: psychological and social components of treatment have strong influences on outcome.

■ The delivery system of long-term prescribing may act to bring order into the lives of chaotic opiate users – whether this is picking up daily from a chemist or (as in the American way) attending a maintenance programme daily.

■ Stimson and Oppenheimer made a valid obsevation when they noted that: 'the clinic system, with its ...constraints, the socially organised policies, treatments and controls, enabled some people to lead stable lives. Stabilisation is, then, not just about drugs, but is about being integrated into a socially engineered system for obtaining them.'[15]

■ Drug workers, like many clients, can be so locked in to 'chemical thinking' about the drugs themselves that they can ignore or under use non-chemical components of methadone treatment.

■ Making decisions about the treatment of individual clients has to be based as far as possible on both a thorough assessment of what will work for that person and on reliable information about 'what works' in general.

■ Research findings can probably be safely generalised to UK practice and can be used to support decision making.

■ The research supports the conclusion that methadone maintenance is more effective than no treatment or placebo in retaining people in treatment, reducing use of heroin and other illicit drugs and reducing involvement in criminal activity and imprisonment rates.

■ Detoxification alone is seldom effective in producing long-term change.

■ Six months after in-patient detoxification and psycho-social treatment in a specialist NHS unit about 50% of opiate addicts are opiate free: treatment in a less expert setting results in poorer outcomes.

■ In-patient detoxification over 10 days is likely to be more distressing, but equally as successful as 21 day detoxification.

■ The benefits of methadone maintenance treatment last as long as maintenance lasts. For some people the long-term benefits can be as great as those of residential rehabilitation.

■ Benefits can be maximised by retaining clients in treatment, prescribing higher rather than lower doses of methadone, orientating programmes towards maintenance rather than abstinence, offering counselling, therapy, and social treatments and the use of contracts and counselling to reduce the use of additional drugs.

section **3**

Methadone

manufacture

and the

preparations

available

Regulations covering methadone manufacture	**32**
Oral methadone preparations available	**32**
Injectable methadone	**34**
Pros and cons of the various oral preparations	**34**
Summary	**37**

Introduction

Methadone can be made in liquid, tablet and injectable forms. This section looks at the law and regulations surrounding methadone and describes the different products that are available and their relative merits.

Regulations covering methadone manufacture

Methadone is usually prescribed as a generic medicine. This means that within the specified constraints of the:

- Drug
- Route of administration
- Concentration

the pharmacist decides which formulation to dispense.

Pharmacists can dispense a ready made product or make it up themselves. This is called 'extemporaneous production'. In the case of methadone mixture this is done by mixing methadone concentrate and diluent.

Manufacture of methadone, as with all medicines, is covered by the Medicines Act. Before a manufacturer can make any claims about, or advertise, a medicine they must have a product licence. Some pharmaceutical companies can, under the terms of their Medicines Control Act manufacturing licence, produce products to be dispensed at the specific request of a doctor under what is called a 'special licence'. Manufacturers of products with a special licence are not allowed to make any claims about their product or advertise them.

There are several companies with licences to manufacture methadone mixture, methadone concentrates and injectable methadone and several more manufacturing them under special licence.

Doctors can (and often do) prescribe drugs outside the terms of the product licence (such as the use of clonidine for opiate detox) or prescribe a drug which has no product licence. When prescribing such products the doctor takes full responsibility for the efficacy and safety of the drug rather than the company that manufactured it.

Oral methadone preparations available

Oral methadone comes in both liquid and tablet form.

Terminology

The terminology used to describe liquid preparations has been the source of much confusion among both workers and clients.

Methadone 1mg/1mL is not a linctus preparation (see below). Methadone 1mg/1mL is known and prescribed as:

- Methadone mixture DTF
- Methadone mixture
- Methadone oral solution
- Martindale methadone mixture.

Methadone mixture DTF1mg/1mL

The treatment of choice for illicit opiate users is methadone mixture 1mg/1mL.[50]

There are several manufacturers making a green 1mg/1mL syrup based on the Drug Tariff Formulary (DTF) formulation:

- Methadone Hydrochloride (HCL) BP 1mg/1mL
- Glucose syrup
- Green S (E142)
- Tartrazine (E102)
- Sunset Yellow (E110)
- Parabens (preservative)
- Ethanol
- Trace chloroform water.

Until early 1995 most of the methadone mixture DTF 1mg/1mL was made by a single manufacturer, however since then a number of manufacturers have started producing DTF formulations. This means that, from time to time, the colour, flavour and/or consistency of the methadone dispensed may change.

If this occurs the reason should be explained to the clients to avoid them becoming anxious about the efficacy of their methadone (which is, of course, unaffected by the taste or consistancy of the liquids used to dissolve the methadone concentrate).

Doctors can prevent the dispensed formulation changing by prescribing methadone for their patients as the proprietary medicine 'Martindale methadone mixture 1mg/1mL'.

Locally prepared methadone mixture1mg/1mL
Pharmacists preparing methadone 1mg/1mL extemporaneously commonly use formulae like the ones below:

Methadone mixture 1mg/mL per 5mL
Methadone HCL BP 5mg
Colourings
Unpreserved syrup 2.5mLs
Double strength chloroform to 5mLs

Methadone mixture 1mg/mL sugar free[51]
Methadone HCL BP 5mg
Concentrated chloroform water 0.1mL
Sorbitol syrup 2mLs
Distilled water to 5mLs

Sugar free and colouring free methadone mixture 1mg/1mL
There are a number of manufacturers making preparations that are:
- Sugar free
- Colouring free
- Sugar and colouring free.

Some of these have a product licence and some are made under special licence.

Methadone linctus 2mg/5mL
Methadone linctus is often confused with methadone mixture by both drug users and doctors. It is a generic medicine which is licensed in the UK for treating coughing in terminal disease but not drug dependence.

Wellcome's methadone preparation 'Physeptone Linctus' is no longer available in the UK. Physeptone linctus is used for the treatment of drug dependence in the Republic of Ireland.

Methadone linctus is rarely used in the UK for the treatment of opiate dependence – and when it is it is often because it has been prescribed by mistake.

A typical formulation of methadone linctus would be:
- Methadone HCL BP 2mg/5mL
- Sucrose BP
- Glycerol BP
- Chloroform BP
- Ethanol
- Caramel BPC 1973
- Flavouring IFF 1831
- Purified water BP
- Benzoates (preservatives).

It is usually dispensed as a clear, brown syrup-based mixture from a 500mL bottle.

Methadone 5mg tablets
The 5mg tablet is most often prescribed under its trade name Physeptone. Physeptone tablets are not licensed for the treatment of opiate dependence. Several companies make generic 5mg tablets. The prescription of methadone in tablet form is discouraged because the tablets:
- Can be crushed and injected
- Have a higher illicit market value (because they can not be diluted)
- Are not as flexible in dose reductions as a liquid preparation.

Physeptone tablets contain:
- Methadone HCL 5mg
- Starch
- Magnesium stearate
- Glycerine.

Other tablet preparations will have similar ingredients. Physeptone tablets are a small, round, white tablet, scored and with 'Wellcome 4LA' written on them. They come in packs of 50.

Methadone suppositories

Methadone can be prepared as a suppository under the special licensing system. They are rarely used in the treatment of dependency. Although they would be expected to have a rapid onset of action the possible therapeutic benefits of this would probably be outweighed by the ease with which they dissolve in water and could thus be injected.

Injectable methadone

There is a range of injectable methadone preparations with a product licence for treatment of dependence. They come at a concentration of:

- 10mg per 1/mL (1%)

In the following ampoule sizes:

- 1mL (10mg)
- 2mL (20mg)
- 3.5mL (35mg)
- 5mL (50mg)

Under special licence other concentrations are made up to 50mg per mL.

The product licence for injectable methadone specifies that it is for intra-muscular or subcutaneous injection but it is usually prescribed and/or used intravenously.

There is fairly widespread anecdotal evidence of these preparations being painful to inject intravenously, especially at high concentrations. There is also anecdotal evidence of their leaving a bitter taste in the mouth following injection.

Pros and cons of the various oral preparations

Methadone mixture DTF1mg /1mL

Advantages	Disadvantages
Best known (and fully licenced) product	Sugar content associated with tooth decay in long-term users
Well accepted by clients	Now produced by several manufacturers so taste/ consistency many vary
Green colour is: a) easy to identify b) difficult to mistake for anything else – which helps prevent accidental overdose	Tartrazine can cause allergic reaction in sensitive people (this is rare and is more likely to occur in clients with asthma)
Unlikely to be injected because a) the chloroform is painful if injected b) the volume and viscosity makes injection inefficient	Large volumes can make storage difficult for both pharmacy and client
Causes vein damage if injected (useful if it stops people injecting)	Causes vein damage if injected (harmful if people inject anyway)
High sugar content means clients like the taste	Sugar content and bright colour may attract children with the attendant risk of accidental overdose
Large volume per mg means it looks like a large dose	May interfere with control of diabetes
Can be bought pre-packed in commonly dispensed volumes	Some clients maintain that it causes weight gain
Long shelf life: 36 months	Large volume to take – especially for people on high doses

Other preparations of methadone oral solution

Advantages

Can be tailor-made for individual clients in terms of dose, volume and concentration

Can be sugar free

Can be free of artificial colourings

If more concentrated than 1mg/1mL reduced volume is easier to store and less to drink

May be cheaper to buy in than ready mixed preparations

Disadvantages

It is difficult to gain the confidence of clients who often doubt the accuracy of production

Time consuming to make up

Can be confused with other medicines or thought not to be methadone if user expects it to be green

Increased risk of accidental overdose especially if concentrations are greater than 1mg/1mL

Reduced volume often not accepted by clients

Some products taste unpleasant

No stability information – limited shelf life

Methadone linctus 2mg/5mL

Advantages

As it is very dilute the large volume looks like a large dose

It could be useful in detox to reduce the dose very slowly

Unlikely to be injected

Clients from the Republic of Ireland often prefer it as it is prescribed there in the same way that methadone mixture is used in the UK

Disadvantages

Sugar content associated with tooth decay and weight gain in long-term users

Colourings and flavourings are associated with allergies

Large volume per mg means people may have to drink large quantities and it may make storage difficult

A pharmacist can mix methadone to any concentration anyway without the expense of buying linctus

There is no product licence for linctus to be used in treatment of drug dependence

5 mg tablets (such as Physeptone)

Advantages	Disadvantages
Clients often prefer tablet preparations	They can be crushed and injected
They can not be spilt/lost as easily as a fluid and can therefore be more convenient when travelling or going on holiday	They have a higher black market value
Clients report reduced nausea on tablets as compared to methadone mixture, and they are easy to swallow with no after taste	The vomiting and nausea cited by most clients requesting tablets is rarely genuine – it is much more likely to be caused by alcohol or a medical problem
Very stable in storage	Easy to store and take discreetly in social situations e.g. work or on holiday
Less bulky than methadone mixture to store	Small unit dose means that people can be taking many pills each day
For private patients paying pharmacy fees it is an inexpensive formulation	Not licensed for, and use discouraged in, treating opiate dependence

summary

■ Methadone is a generic medicine – not a brand name.

■ Methadone mixture 1mg/1mL is the treatment of choice when prescribing for opiate users.

■ The majority of people on methadone are given oral methadone mixture DTF 1mg/1mL but there are a number of other products and formulation variants available, although these may be poorly accepted by clients.

■ Different liquid formulations only alter the medium in which the methadone is dissolved and will therefore have the same effect on the client.

■ There are a number of manufacturers producing methadone mixture and methadone concentrate.

■ Methadone linctus is a much weaker preparation (2mg/5mL) that is seldom used in the treatment of dependence and should not be confused with methadone mixture 1mg/ 1mL.

■ Prescribing methadone in tablet form is rarely justified and is best avoided if possible.

■ Injectable methadone comes in a variety of strengths. It is usually prescribed only by specialist doctors and is designed for intramuscular or subcutaneous use although it is often administered intravenously.

section 4

Physiology and pharmacology of methadone

The chemistry of methadone	40
The effects of methadone	40
Opiate effects on the central nervous system	41
Opiate effects on the peripheral nervous system	44
Histamine release-related effects	45
Other reported effects	46
Effects on babies	47
Things that methadone does not cause	49
Long-term effects	50
Dental decay	50
Methadone metabolism	51
Tolerance	56
Methadone overdose	57
Treatment of methadone overdose	58
Withdrawal symptoms and their causes	59
Drug interactions	60
Medical conditions and methadone	62
Summary	64

Introduction

Methadone, as with all opiates, is a relatively simple compound that has a powerful and complex range of effects on those who take it. But the degree of effect, and the subjective experience, can vary widely between individuals.

This section looks at the effects of methadone on the brain and body, how the body responds to the presence of methadone and how tolerance develops. There is also information on what methadone is and how it interacts with other drugs.

As the issue of how to equate methadone dose with illicit drug use is as much a matter of policy, practice, assessment and local trends as a matter of physiology and pharmacology, it is dealt with in Section 8 – Getting the starting dose right.

The chemistry of methadone

Methadone hydrochloride consists of:
- Carbon: 21 atoms
- Hydrogen: 27 atoms
- Nitrogen: 1 atom
- Oxygen: 1 atom
- Hydrochloride

$$\blacksquare HCL$$

$$CH_3CH_2COC\underset{\displaystyle C_6H_5}{\overset{\displaystyle C_6H_5}{|}}{-}CH_2CH\overset{\displaystyle N(CH_3)_2}{|}CH_3$$

The approved name of methadone hydrochloride is:
6-dimethylamino-4,4-diphenyl-3-hepatone hydrochloride.

The methadone molecule can be drawn like this:

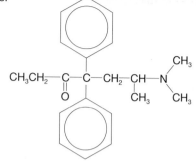

There appear to be two separate active sites in the molecule:
- The nitrogen atom with the hydrochloride bonded to it at one end – thought to act on the peripheral nervous system
- The 2 phenyl 'rings' which are thought to be necessary for its opiate-like action on the central nervous system.

Methadone is:
- A white crystalline powder
- It melts at 233–236°C.

It is soluble in:
- 1 in 12 of water
- 1 in 7 of ethanol
- 1 in 3 of chloroform
It does not dissolve in ether.

The effects of methadone

Until the intricate workings of the nervous system are fully understood the precise causes of all the effects of opiates cannot be explained. However extensive studies, experiments, and clinical experience together give us a clear indication of the effects of these drugs and the mechanisms that cause these effects.

Opiates appear to share some of the properties, and mimic the action of some groups of the body's naturally occurring chemicals called peptides, in particular:
- Endorphins
- Enkephalines
- Dynorphins.

Studies of the binding of opiates and these peptides to specific sites in the brain and other organs have suggested the existence of as many as 8 types of opioid receptors which, in addition, may all have sub-type receptors.[52]

Opiates directly cause a number of actions which can be divided into the following groups:
■ Opiate effects on the central nervous system (CNS)
■ Opiate effects on the peripheral nervous system
■ Opiate induced histamine release-related effects
■ Other reported effects for which there is no identified and/or proven causal effect
■ Effects on the unborn foetus.

The effects in each of these categories are listed below. Following the lists there are explanations, where possible, of the mechanisms involved.

Opiate effects on the central nervous system
■ Euphoria
■ Pleasant, warm feeling in the stomach
■ Pain relief
■ Drowsiness
■ Sleep
■ Nausea
■ Vomiting
■ Respiratory depression (rate and depth of breathing reduced)
■ Cough reflex depression
■ Arms and legs feeling heavy
■ Convulsions (caused by high doses only and very rare with methadone)

Opiate effects on the peripheral nervous system
■ Dryness of the mouth, eyes and nose
■ Constipation
■ Small pupils
■ Difficulty passing urine

Histamine release-related effects
■ Itching
■ Sweating
■ Blushing
■ Flushing of the skin
■ Constricting of the airways

Other reported associated effects for which there is either no identified or proven causal effect
■ Reduced or absent menstrual cycle
■ Altered sexual desire
■ Hallucinations
■ Swelling of feet and ankles
■ Delayed orgasm
■ Difficulty controlling orgasm
■ Heart pounding
■ Anxiety
■ Weight gain

Effects on the foetus and young child
■ Low birth weight
■ Withdrawal symptoms

The mechanism thought to be responsible for each of these catagories of effects is described below.

Opiate effects on the central nervous system

Euphoria
Feelings of euphoria are not universally experienced. Heroin users often report that the euphoric effects of methadone are not nearly as pronounced as those of heroin. This is to be expected, to some extent, as heroin is smoked or injected and thus has a much quicker onset of action than oral methadone. However many drug users report that even injected methadone produces a qualitatively different euphoria to that of heroin.

The feeling 'on methadone' is often described as simply absence of withdrawal symptoms but the increase in anxiety, stress and psychological discomfort experienced by many users on detoxification programmes suggests that the methadone is contributing

41

to a sense of relief from distress – even if this is not experienced as pronounced euphoria.

The mechanism by which opiates produce a sense of euphoria and tranquillity is not yet agreed. It may be partly via action on a part of the brain called the locus cerulus. The locus cerulus has high concentrations of opioid receptors and is thought to play a crucial role in feelings of alarm, panic, fear and anxiety.[52]

In any event the neural systems that cause the feeling of euphoria appear to be different from the systems that cause physical dependence and pain relief.[53]

In theory as the dose of opiates is increased the euphoric effect rises. However some long-term methadone users have taken near-fatal doses and still reported that the high was nothing like that of heroin. It is likely that some methadone overdoses are the result of people trying to achieve a heroin-like euphoria using a drug which is apparently unable to produce these same feelings.

In experiments using people who are pain free with no history of opiate use not all experience a pleasant effect. Some experience a dysphoria[52]: uncomfortable, disorientated feelings which can be made worse by the feelings of nausea which are common.

Pleasant, warm feeling in the stomach
As with all opiates, this is a reported effect that accompanies the euphoria. The mechanisms involved are not understood.

Pain relief
Opiates reduce pain through a number of mechanisms (described below) but although the pain relief is often only partial they also alter the perception of painful stimuli and thus make pain more tolerable.

Opiates do not alter the sensitivity of nerve endings to pain, rather they interfere with the transmission of signals via the nervous system to the brain. They do this by:
■ Decreasing conduction along the nerves that run between the nerve endings and the spine
■ Preventing production of the chemicals that allow signals to pass between the nerves and the spinal cord
■ Stimulating production of serotonin (also known as 5HT) and noradrenaline (also known as norepinephrine) which significantly reduces pain signals reaching the brain
■ Mimicking the action of endorphins at their receptor sites.

Through their action in the spinal column they reduce the ability of the body to produce reflex actions to painful stimuli.

The ability of opiates to inhibit the body's response to stimuli is selective in that they do not affect touch, vibration, vision or hearing.

Drowsiness
Opiates cause some sedation, although in clients taking a dose to which they are tolerant, on a daily basis, drowsiness caused by methadone is unlikely.

Opiate users develop tolerance to the clouding of thought which may be related to drowsiness. Other related effects which are reported in studies of opiate use in volunteers with no history of opiate use are:
■ Inability to concentrate
■ Apathy
■ Reduced physical activity
■ Lethargy
■ Reduced visual acuity.

It is important to look at other possible causes when these symptoms are found in long-term methadone users before they are attributed to the methadone.

At the start of methadone treatment clients should be warned that methadone causes sedation, and of the possibility that it may impair co-ordination and the ability to perform skilled tasks such as driving. This is especially marked (and can cause overdose) when other central nervous system depressants such as alcohol or benzodiazepines are also taken.[54]

Sleep

Of those clients who can take their methadone home most usually take part of their methadone late in the evening to help them sleep. Many drug users lack a natural sleep pattern so they use methadone as a trigger to initiate sleep.

Methadone's action at the opioid receptors results in sedation and mood changes, which are more marked in the initial hours after dosing when the blood concentrations are marginally higher. But blood concentrations vary little in regular methadone users so the association with sleep is probably mostly psychological.

The sleep-promoting effects of methadone may be particularly important for people with underlying anxiety.

Some clients report persistent problems with sleep although how much of this is due to methadone and how much is due to:
■ Drug use becoming more stable since starting methadone treatment
■ Instability of drug use
■ Unrealistic expectations of the sleep-inducing properties of methadone
■ Previously unrecognised poor sleep pattern
■ Underlying anxiety or other mental health problems
is often a useful topic for discussion between worker and client.

Nausea and vomiting

The feelings of nausea associated with opiates are partly due to direct stimulation of the chemo-receptor trigger zone (CTZ) in the part of the brain known as the medulla.

Not everyone is susceptible to CTZ stimulation by opiates and tolerance builds, albeit sometimes slowly, for those who are.

Vomiting caused by methadone is rare. Most in-patient methadone dose titration services rarely, if ever, encounter people who vomit their methadone dose. Services which prescribe only methadone mixture usually find that clients are able to tolerate this despite protestations to the contrary at the outset of treatment.

People who vomit methadone usually do so for reasons independent of the methadone. Far more likely causes of vomiting are:
■ Excessive alcohol use
■ Eating large meals
■ Pre-existing eating disorder
■ Pre-existing stomach problems e.g. ulcer.

All of these can be exacerbated by CTZ stimulation and the slowing of the movement of the intestine by methadone (see opiate effects on the peripheral nervous system below).

Vomiting as a side effect of methadone is often reported at assessment - usually accompanying a request for methadone in tablet or injectable form.

Even if the other causes for vomiting listed above have been excluded you must be satisfied that the nausea and vomiting are genuine before considering alternative preparations because the request for tablet form methadone may arise either from a desire to crush and inject the tablets or an intention to sell the tablets.

If treatment with an oral methadone solution is chosen it is usually best to either commence treatment in an observed environment or to start treatment with a guarantee to review in a week. Almost always the client will stabilise and not find vomiting to be as problematic as they expected.

Respiratory depression

Respiratory depression is partly caused by a direct inhibitory effect on the brain stem respiratory centres which normally increase the breathing when the level of carbon dioxide in the blood rises.

Opiates also depress the action of the centres that regulate the breathing rhythm. These effects are not normally significant other than in overdose where respiratory arrest is the most common cause of death.[55]

Respiratory depression, coupled with a high incidence of smoking, can result in opiate users presenting with chronic and/or serious chest infections. Staff should be alert to this risk as early intervention can prevent extensive use of antibiotics and serious illness.

Cough reflex suppression

Opiates also have a direct suppressant effect on the cough centre in the medulla which is partly responsible for triggering a cough in response to irritation of the lower airways.[19]

Arms and legs feeling heavy

The cause of this subtle, but not unpleasant, effect of methadone is not understood. It may result from the effect of methadone on the nerve pathways, coupled with the increased blood flow to the peripheral blood vessels.

Convulsions

Doses far in excess of the normal therapeutic range of opiates can cause convulsions. This is therefore theoretically possible with methadone although there is no published evidence of this happening. There appear to be several mechanisms involved when convulsions occur in exciting certain groups of brain cells and in suppressing the production of chemicals that normally keep brain activity within safe limits.

Naloxone is effective in treating convulsions caused by methadone. Diazepam may also be an effective treatment. Anti-convulsants may not be effective.

See also the notes on epilepsy at the end of this section under 'Medical conditions and methadone'.

Opiate effects on the peripheral nervous system

Methadone has a powerful effect on the peripheral nervous system. This may be as a result of an inhibitory effect on some opiate receptors[55].

The effects of opiates on the peripheral nervous system seem to be more resistant to the development of tolerance than the other effects.

Dryness of the mouth, eyes and nose

All opiate drugs reduce secretion of saliva, tears and mucous in the respiratory tract by blocking the receptors that need to be stimulated for the production of these secretions.

Constipation

The waves of muscular contraction that propel the stomach contents through the large bowel can be virtually stopped by methadone. Indeed opiates are so good at slowing the passage of food through the gut that they can be used in the treatment of dysentery!

Methadone also reduces the normal stimuli to defecate and increases the tone of the anal sphincter muscle which further contributes to the constipation that is almost universal among methadone users.

A high-fibre diet and a high (non alcohol) fluid intake are the best methods for reducing constipation.

Nausea

Opiates reduce the movement of the stomach and both movement and size of the duodenum by causing the muscles to contract. This can delay the passage of food through the small bowel by as much as 12 hours. This may increase feelings of nausea (see above) by contributing to a feeling of being 'full' even several hours after eating.

Small pupils (miosis)

Opiates probably stimulate the oculomotor nerve causing the iris to contract leaving only a small hole for light to pass through. Tolerance to this effect of opiates is only partial – even after long-term use.

Because of this the degree of pupil constriction is a reliable indicator of the level of opiates in a person's blood stream [55].

Difficulty passing urine

This is a less commonly experienced effect.

Opiates can increase the tone of the sphincter muscles that allow urine to pass from the bladder thus making it more difficult to relax them in order to pass urine.

This can be aggravated by the methadone also making the bladder contract more strongly causing 'urinary urgency'.

Histamine release-related effects

In the blood, lungs, intestines, etc. there is a type of cell called a mast cell. Its function is to recognise 'invaders' in the blood and to attack them.

On encountering a substance to which the mast cell is sensitive it ruptures, releasing histamine. Histamine is the main agent in the body's allergic response. It has a number of effects, all of which are supposed to be helpful in attacking an invading substance to which the body is sensitive. Histamine triggers the opening up of the tiny blood vessels in the skin which produces:
- Blushing
- Flushing of the skin
- Itching
- Sweating.

It also causes:
- Constricting of the airways.

The opening of the blood vessels near the surface increases the number of white blood cells near a likely source of further attack. Constriction of the airway may serve some purpose in reducing the number of foreign bodies that can be inhaled. All of these effects can be exacerbated by anxiety.

Mast cell sensitivity to substances can be helpful, for instance in attacking bacteria, or unhelpful, for instance when it causes the hay fever reaction to pollen.

Methadone (and other opiate) molecules are able to enter mast cells and cause them to release histamine - with the above effects. But it is not an allergic reaction because it is caused by the molecule entering the cell rather than by the mast cell 'recognising' methadone as a foreign substance[55]. It is not something that people develop a tolerance to.

Sweating

Sweating is a common long-term problem in methadone users and histamine release may be partly to blame. However the fact that it can be so severe, and that it is often present in the absence of other histamine-related effects, indicates that there may well be other, not yet understood, mechanisms at work.

Other reported effects

There are a number of other effects that are associated with methadone for which there is no clear and/or proven causal mechanism. The list has been compiled from anecdotal evidence and reports in the literature.

These effects occur in people who take methadone and in the general population. Where we have found a suggested mechanism linking methadone to the effect, it is described.

Reduced or absent menstrual cycle

This is the most commonly reported experience in this category. There are other causes of amenorrhoea (absence of periods) such as stress and poor nutrition which may well contribute to the problem.

Levels of the hormones that control menstruation, follicle stimulating hormone and luteinising hormone, remain normal in women receiving long-term high doses of methadone,[52] and amenorrhoea is not recognised as an effect of opiate treatment for other pain relief. However there are a large number of anecdotal reports of the normal menstrual cycle resuming during or post methadone detox, a time when stress levels are likely to be high and appetite poor.

All women taking methadone should be advised that even if their periods have stopped they may still become pregnant.

Altered sexual desire

All opiates are considered to reduce sexual desire. A minority of methadone users report persistent reduced sexual function. The cause of this reduced desire is not known but the sentiment 'when you've got opiates you don't need sex' is common among opiate users and may point simply to an under reporting of sexual activity – which is no longer highly valued – rather than levels of sexual activity which are less than the general population.

In a small study of 29 people dependent on methadone Cicero et al found that serum testosterone levels of those taking methadone were 43% lower than those of the heroin users and the study control group.[56]

Some methadone users report increased sexual desire as a result of taking methadone. It seems likely that this has as much to do with other factors such as increased stability, reduced stress and alcohol intake, as with any direct pharmacological effect of methadone.

Delayed orgasm and difficulty controlling orgasm

Methadone may cause increased tone in the sphincter muscles that close off the urethra, having the effect, in men, of delaying orgasm. Difficulty controlling orgasm could be a result of increased sensitivity while less sedated on methadone than on heroin.

Hallucinations

The literature describing the effects of opiates in general (from which a lot of information on methadone is extrapolated) often mentions hallucinations as an effect, and heroin users describe a dream-like state when using heroin which can include perceptual alterations. But with the slower onset and reduced intensity of methadone it is very unlikely that someone who is being treated for opiate dependence, with no previous history of mental illness, would experience hallucinations due to methadone.

Swelling of feet and ankles

This is a rare transient reaction at the commencement of methadone prescribing. It usually goes within a few weeks of the start of treatment. The cause is not known.

Heart pounding

This has been reported as a transient effect when plasma levels of methadone reach a peak, about 4 hours after an oral dose.[57] The cause is not known and it is rarely problematic.

Anxiety

Again this is an effect extrapolated from the literature on other opiates as some people do not find the experience of opiates pleasant. However methadone users are a self selected group who have enjoyed the experience of taking opiates.

Increased anxiety could have a number of causes such as:
- Underlying anxiety disorder
- Insufficient methadone dose
- Benzodiazepine withdrawals
- Alcohol withdrawals
- Having more time while on methadone due to no longer having the distractions that were related to daily heroin use.

The experience of many opiate users is of reduced anxiety during methadone treatment.

Weight gain

The calorific value of methadone mixture DTF is only 1.7 kilo calories/mL.[58] This makes a dose of 50mg (85 kilo calories) equivalent to eating just a couple of biscuits so it is unlikely that the weight gain sometimes reported as linked to methadone is due to its calorific value.

Other factors could include:
- Increased appetite on methadone in relation to appetite on heroin
- Poor diet
- Client being underweight at start of treatment
- Reduced physical activity
- Reduced stress.

Effects on babies

In Section 11: Prescribing for groups with special needs, there is further discussion on:
- Care of the pregnant woman
- Other risks to the foetus (which are often greater than the risk from the methadone)
- Care of the newborn baby.

Overall risk to babies of women using prescribed methadone

No increased level of congenital abnormalities has been observed in the babies of women who have taken methadone during their pregnancy.

47

The problems listed below look alarming when put together but they should be read in conjunction with their explanatory notes and in the overall context of the risk assessment scale of a standard text on the subject *Drugs in pregnancy and lactation: a reference guide to foetal and neonatal risk*.[59]

Normal methadone treatment is rated:
'**Risk category B:**
...no controlled studies in pregnant women or animal studies have shown an adverse effect...in women in the first trimester and there is no evidence of risk in later trimesters.'

It has been suggested that the withdrawal syndrome from heroin in babies is less prevalent and less severe than methadone withdrawal syndrome and that it may be safer for mothers to take heroin up to delivery – particularly if they smoke the drug – than methadone. Although this may be true the current consensus is that in the vast majority of cases the other risks associated with illicit drug use such as overdose, sudden withdrawals, adulterants, crime, etc. are likely to outweigh the benefits of potentially milder withdrawals for the baby following delivery.

This is supported by *Drugs in pregnancy and lactation* which rates methadone treatment for 'prolonged periods' or 'in high doses at term' as:

'**Risk category D:**

There is positive evidence of human foetal risk, but the benefits from use in pregnant women may be acceptable despite the risk...'

If methadone substitution (either on a reducing or maintenance basis) can help alleviate the drug-related risks and improve ante-natal care (through increased contact with services) then it is a positive intervention.

Possible problems following methadone use during pregnancy

The main problems appear to be:

- Low birth weight
- Withdrawal symptoms in the baby.

Some studies have also found raised incidence of jaundice, Sudden Infant Death Syndrome and raised mortality. All of these possible problems are discussed below, and should be read in conjunction with the notes above.

Low birthweight

There is an increased incidence of low birth weight in babies born to opiate-using mothers. Johnstone[60] quotes 11 studies which together covered nearly 1200 babies delivered to mothers whose main or only drug was methadone, which show that about 25% of babies had a low birth weight.

The babies of women taking only methadone may have a higher birthweight than comparable babies of women taking only heroin[61] – but whether this is due to differences in the drugs or other differences is unclear.

It has been suggested that low birth weight is due to heroin having an effect on the growth of the unborn child.[62] Even if this is true (and there is no proof that it is) there are a number of other factors that are often present in opiate users that are known to contribute to low birth weight:

- Premature delivery
- Poor nutrition
- Poverty
- Smoking tobacco.

The neonatal withdrawal syndrome

Between 42% and 95%[63] of babies of opiate-using mothers may experience a withdrawal syndrome.

Neonatal withdrawal syndrome is not always directly related to the amount of opiates the mother is taking nor to the amount of opiates in the baby's blood. It normally starts within 48 hours of delivery, but in a small percentage of cases may be delayed for 7–14 days.

Withdrawal symptoms in babies

Symptoms commonly associated with neonatal opiate withdrawal are:

- Irritability and sleep disturbance
- Sneezing
- Fist sucking
- A shrill cry
- Watery stools
- General hyperactivity
- Ineffectual sucking
- Poor weight gain
- Dislike of bright lights.

Symptoms less commonly associated with opiate withdrawal are:

- Yawning
- Vomiting
- Increased mucus production
- Increased response to sound
- And, rarely, convulsions.

Other problems in the newborn that have been associated with methadone use

Other problems that have been reported by some studies as occurring more frequently in the babies of women who are methadone dependent than in the general population are:
■ Infant mortality
■ Sudden Infant Death Syndrome (SIDS/cot death)
■ Jaundice.

Studies often caution that many of the women in their samples have used a variety of drugs during pregnancy and that it is difficult to separate the effects of methadone from the effects of these other drugs.

The modest increase in mortality of babies born to drug-using (i.e. not always just methadone-using) mothers is due to premature birth[60] and stillbirth in late pregnancy. However there are two factors which may limit the extent to which these studies are relevant: firstly most studies were carried out in the 1970s when the perinatal mortality rate was higher and many were carried out in the USA where health care is very different from that in the UK.

A link between drug addiction and Sudden Infant Death Syndrome (SIDS) has been suggested by a study of 702 infants in which 20 babies died (2.8%) but the authors could not attribute the increase to a single drug.[59] Another study of 313 babies[61] found no increased prevalence of SIDS from that in the locality. These studies were carried out before the practice of laying babies on their backs to help prevent SIDS became widespread.

Jaundice is comparatively infrequent in the babies of both heroin and methadone-using mothers. It is treatable and usually passes, without harm to the baby.

Respiratory depression at birth

This is not a significant problem for babies born to opiate-tolerant mothers receiving methadone treatment. Studies consistently find that the APGAR scores (the standard measurement of physical well-being at birth) of babies born to women using methadone are comparable to the general population.

Things that methadone does not cause

There are a number of things which methadone does not do which merit listing as they are often assumed (by both drug users and professionals) to be inevitable effects of long-term opiate use.

Therapeutic doses of methadone do not cause:
■ Damage to any of the major organs or systems of the body – even in high dose, long-term use
■ Significant inco-ordination
■ Slurred speech
■ Congenital abnormalities in unborn children (see above)
■ Reductions in cognitive ability in the way alcohol does.

nor does it:
■ Have any anti-convulsant effect – even at high doses
■ Effect levels of leuteinising and follicle stimulating hormones in women.[52]

Long-term effects

The long-term toxic side effects of methadone (in fact all pharmaceutical opiates), if taken in hygienic conditions and in controlled doses, are few and (relative to the risks of alcohol, tobacco or illicit heroin use) benign.

Since the mid 1960s there have been about 1.5 million person years of methadone maintenance in the US alone and there have been thousands of carefully documented research cases[64] which support M J Kreek's conclusion that:
'**Physiological and biochemical alterations occur, but there are minimal side effects that are clinically detectable in patients during chronic methadone maintenance treatment. Toxicity related to methadone during chronic treatment is extraordinarily rare. The most important medical consequence during chronic treatment, in fact, is the marked improvement in the general health and nutrition status observed in patients as compared with their status at the time of admission to treatment.**'[65]

The main long-term problems caused, as described below, are tooth decay, constipation and accidental overdose.

Dental decay

Methadone has traditionally come as a syrup-based mixture. Prolonged contact with this sugary liquid has been associated with tooth decay and dental caries, especially towards the front of the mouth.

53% of methadone users on methadone mixture report problematic side effects such as dental problems.[66] There are 3 ways that methadone mixture can contribute to decay:
■ The high sugar content causes the growth of plaque
■ The acidic nature of the liquid can cause direct corrosion of the enamel

■ Methadone inhibits saliva production and saliva is one of the body's natural defences against plaque.

However there are other possible causes for dental problems in methadone users, such as:
■ Pre-existing dental problems
■ High sugar diet
■ Poor oral hygiene.

Also:
■ Methadone is an analgesic which can mask toothache
■ Heroin is also a powerful analgesic so toothache may only start to be felt when the user is stabilised on methadone
■ Cocaine users also on methadone rub cocaine into their gums to test its purity. Cocaine results in numbness and contaminants damage the surrounding teeth.

Researchers have noticed similar prevalence of dental problems in intravenous heroin users who are not on methadone. This supports the conclusion that poor dental health is endemic among opiate users and that methadone may be exacerbating pre-existing problems rather than causing new ones.[67]

Prevention of tooth decay
Dentists recommend using aqueous-based, sugar-free methadone, especially in long-term methadone treatment. However, more importantly they advise informing users of methadone's potential to harm their teeth and the importance of:
■ Low sugar diet
■ Good dental hygiene
■ Regular check-ups
■ Brushing their teeth
■ Rinsing the mouth immediately after taking methadone
■ Taking methadone mixture through a straw.

Methadone metabolism

Methadone is soluble in body fats called lipids, so it is well absorbed from the gastrointestinal tract into the blood stream. It is primarily broken down in the liver and undergoes fairly extensive metabolism as it passes through the liver for the first time.

It binds very well to albumin and other plasma proteins and also (without causing damage) to various body tissues, especially to the:

- Lungs
- Kidneys
- Liver
- Spleen.

The concentration of methadone in these organs is much higher than in the blood.

There is then a fairly slow transfer of methadone between these stores in the tissues and the blood. For methadone to be active it must be contained in the blood so it can travel to the brain. Even if there are extensive stores elsewhere in the body a client will only feel the effects of methadone actually in the blood.

Methadone metabolites are eliminated in the urine and faeces together with unchanged methadone (about 10% of the methadone administered orally is excreted unchanged).[70] It is also secreted in sweat and saliva.

Methadone is found in high concentrations in gastric juices. During pregnancy the concentration in the placental cord blood is about half the maternal level.

Half-life

The half-life of a drug is the name given to the time it takes for blood levels of a drug to drop to 50% of the peak concentration. The half-life of diamorphine (heroin) is around 3 minutes. The half-life of methadone depends upon whether it is a first dose or a dose given as part of an ongoing programme.

Single, first dose

The apparent half-life of a single oral dose of methadone is shorter than that in extended use. This is because much of the initial dose becomes distributed into the tissue reservoirs and is therefore not available in the blood stream.

Following ingestion of oral methadone blood levels rise for about 4 hours and then begin to fall. The apparent half-life of a single first dose is 12–18 hours with a mean average of 15 hours.[68]

Single dose of oral methadone

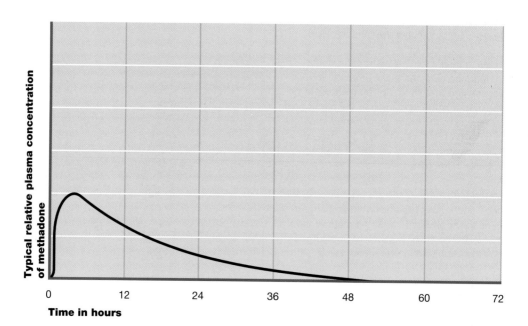

Typical relative plasma concentration of methadone

Time in hours

0   12   24   36   48   60   72

First few days of usage

Over the first 3 days of methadone consumption the 'tissue reservoirs' of methadone in the lungs, kidneys and liver gradually fills. After the first day subsequent doses start from a higher baseline and therefore reach a higher peak. The half-life of the drug reflects only clearance of the drug from the system and is therefore extended to between 13 and 47 hours with a mean average of 25 hours.[68]

This graph illustrates the 3 days it takes for the 'tissue reservoirs' to fill.

First 3 days of dispensing, for oral methadone, with once-daily dosing (doses at 0, 24, 48 hours)

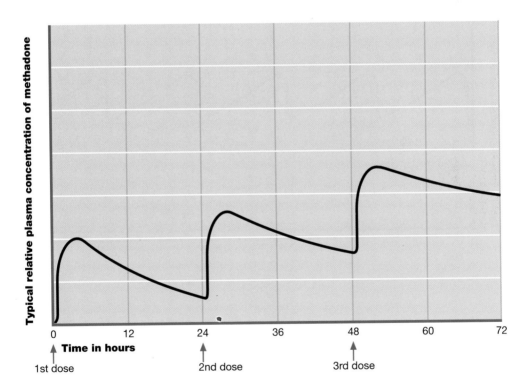

Regular dosing

Once in a steady state variations in blood concentration levels are relatively small. Clients may prefer to take their daily dose at a particular time each day but this makes little difference to their blood levels of methadone.

Methadone's long half-life means that once-daily dosing should theoretically be adequate for clients who have been on a constant oral methadone dose for more than 3 days.

Once-daily dosing of oral methadone at steady state

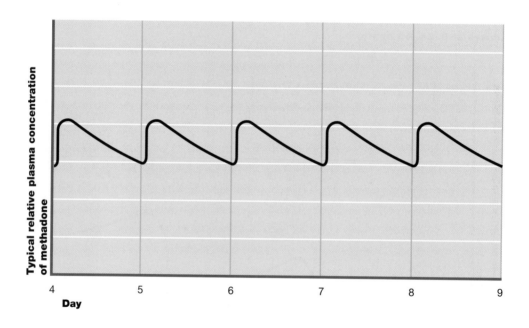

Typical relative plasma concentration of methadone

Day 4   5   6   7   8   9

Missed dose

If one day's dose of methadone is omitted from a regular regime the blood concentration will continue to fall gradually over the 24–48 hour interval.

After 25 hours a person on a regular once-daily dosing regime will have methadone blood levels equal to around half the peak level i.e. 4 hours after dosing. The blood concentration would typically fall to 25% of the peak level after 48 hours.

3 day recovery to steady state from missed dose at day 10

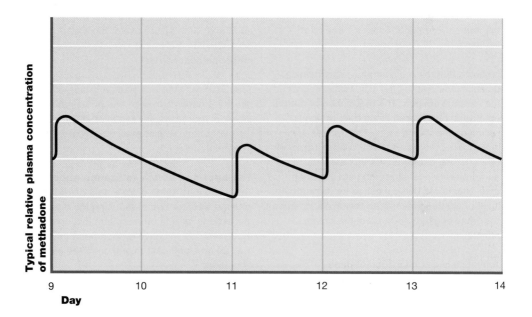

Typical relative plasma concentration of methadone

Day

Tolerance

The tolerance developing mechanisms

After daily exposure to opiates people become tolerant[69], so after a time, the same dose will have a reduced effect on the user.

Tolerance to the different effects that opiates have on the body build up separately – and at different rates – so users may develop complete tolerance to one effect, such as nausea, and virtually none to another, such as constipation.

56

Tolerance to methadone builds very slowly which is one of the reasons it is used in the treatment of drug dependence. The mechanisms that enable tolerance to develop are not fully understood, but we do know that the number of opiate receptors does not increase.

It seems that the brain's natural biochemical balance is altered by the constant presence of the external opiates. The production of natural opioids is suppressed since their action is reduced, and the rate at which opiates are metabolised increases.[50] The concentration of other natural neurotransmitters such as noradrenaline and serotonin rises because their effects are being masked by the high level of opiates present. As the levels increase they may begin to counteract the opiate effects.

Tolerance is a combination of three mechanisms which help the body compensate for the constant presence of opiates:
■ Neuroadaption – changes at the nerve endings
■ Increased metabolism of the drug
■ Learning how to compensate for the effects of the drug.

The speed at which opiate tolerance develops

Tolerance to opiates rises more quickly during second and subsequent exposures to the drug.

Tolerance to opiates can develop within 2 weeks of commencement of daily opiate use. Tolerance to methadone develops more slowly than with many opiates and so is rarely a significant problem. Because it is so long-acting blood levels and response to methadone should become fairly constant.

Manifestations of withdrawal symptoms – or the client feeling that their methadone is not enough whilst on a constant dose – are not always to be related to physical tolerance. Other causes include withdrawal from additional illicit opiate use or increased psychological pressures reducing the effects of the methadone dose.

Tolerance to two of methadone's side-effects, pin-point pupils[68] (miosis) and constipation, develop very slowly indeed (if at all) and both are very often present even after years of treatment.

The speed at which tolerance goes

Tolerance may go as quickly as it develops, so within a week or two of reducing the dose of methadone (or any other opiate) it is possible that tolerance will have dropped and there may be no significant tolerance to the effects of opiates.

This means that people post detox and intermittent users of opiates are at particular risk of overdose.

Cross tolerance

Because opiates act in similar ways withdrawal symptoms can usually be avoided by substituting one for another. This phenomenon is called 'cross tolerance'. The degree of cross tolerance between any two opiate drugs is proportional to the degree of similarity in their sites of action.

An exception to this rule is buprenorphine (Temgesic) which, if substituted for heroin or methadone, can precipitate withdrawals because it excludes them from the receptor sites.

Methadone overdose

In 1992 there were 345 deaths of opiate users attributed directly or indirectly to their opiate use:
- 51 died from heroin overdose
- 131 died from methadone overdose.

Methadone is one of the strongest opiates. It has a slow onset of action and a long half-life and causes severe respiratory depression which is usually the cause of death.

Methadone is relatively available on the illicit market as there are large numbers of tolerant individuals whose daily dose is well over the lethal dose for non-tolerant individuals. This may explain why, of the fatalities above, only 25% had been previously notified to the Home Office, and why methadone overdose deaths among people in treatment are relatively rare.

Dangerous doses
Adults: For non-tolerant adults a dose of 50mg may be fatal.[73] The lethal dose is less if methadone is taken in conjunction with alcohol or other sedatives such as benzodiazepines.

Children: 10mg has been fatal[72] although one child who took 60mg survived. Children are particularly susceptible to the effects of methadone in overdose. Numerous deaths have been reported world-wide.[72] Children require treatment if they consume any amount of methadone.

Prevention of overdose
Methadone should always be supplied and stored in bottles with 'child-resistant' caps. These bottles should be clearly labelled with the risk of overdose if it is taken by anyone other than the person it is prescribed for and the quantity and strength of methadone they contain.

It is important to remember – and tell clients – that even small children can open bottles with 'child-resistant' caps. Bottles containing methadone should therefore never be left in a position where they could possibly be handled by children.

Methadone users who take their methadone home should always be made aware of the risks. The safe storage of the methadone in the home should always be part of the care plan.

Giving the following advice on the prevention of overdose to methadone users from the very beginning of their treatment can save lives:
- Make sure you are not alone for the first 2–4 hours after taking your first dose of prescribed methadone
- If moving from street drugs to a new methadone prescription beware of celebrating this by using street drugs on top of the new prescription
- Do not use other drugs in addition to your methadone on your own – ask someone to stay with you
- Do not mix methadone with alcohol
- Do not mix methadone with tranquillisers or other drugs.

Signs of methadone overdose

- Nausea and vomiting
- Constricted (pin-point) pupils
- Drowsiness
- Cold clammy blue-ish skin
- Reduced heart rate
- Reduced systolic blood pressure
- Reduced body temperature.

If the dose is large enough, and the person is left untreated, this can lead to:

- Breathlessness
- Respiratory depression with cyanosis (turning blue) and apnoea (stopping breathing)
- Pulmonary oedema (fluid gathering in the lungs)
- Possible convulsions due to hypoxia (lack of oxygen)
- Death.

Low doses of methadone mainly reduce respiratory frequency whilst higher doses also diminish tidal volume. This is because methadone blunts the natural respiratory drive mechanisms.[68]

Treatment of methadone overdose

First aid

Methadone overdose is a serious medical emergency. In the event of suspected overdose call an ambulance.

If the person is losing consciousness lie them on their side in the recovery position so that they will not choke if they vomit.

Inducing people to vomit is not recommended because of the risk of rapid onset of CNS depression/unconsciousness which could lead to choking.

Medical treatment

A doctor should give 50g activated charcoal and observe for at least 24 hours.[72]

For children give 10–15g activated charcoal. Non-tolerant adults who have consumed more than 30mg of methadone may need a stomach wash-out. Even after 4 hours a stomach wash-out may be worthwhile because of reduced gut motility caused by the methadone.

Adults who are already prescribed methadone may need a stomach wash-out if they take more than twice their daily dose – depending on their tolerance levels and response. There is anecdotal evidence of people taking in excess of four times their normal daily dose and remaining conscious.

Naloxone (Narcan)

This is a short-acting opiate antagonist used to reverse the effects of methadone in overdose. It works by competing with methadone for opiate receptors in the brain.[74] Naloxone is indicated for use in coma or bradypnoea (very slow breathing) associated with methadone overdose. Repeated increasing doses are required at intervals of 2–3 minutes if respiratory function does not improve. Alternatively an intravenous infusion may be given, the rate of administration being adjusted according to response. The *British National Formulary (BNF)* contains the appropriate dosage regime.

Because methadone has such a long half-life (mean average 15 hours for one-off dose or 25 hours in regular users) naloxone may be needed for prolonged periods after overdose. Even though the patient has recovered s/he may relapse once the effects of naloxone wear off. It is important to try and observe anyone who has severely overdosed for 24 hours. However any dependant opiate user who has had naloxone administered will experience acute withdrawals and will be likely to discharge themself from hospital.

Supplemental therapy

In patients with severe respiratory depression which does not improve with naloxone mechanical ventilation will be necessary.

Diazepam is the drug of choice for convulsions. Hypotension usually responds to intravenous fluids or inotropes.

Withdrawal symptoms and their causes

For discussion of the other issues related to withdrawal symptoms see also:
- Section 2 – The research basis for methadone prescribing
- Section 7 – Treatment choices
- Section 9 – Methadone detoxification.

The mind and body adjust to the constant presence of opiates, reduction in the levels of opiates can create an imbalance as the body reacts to the change. The symptoms of this imbalance are collectively called the withdrawal syndrome.

The only group of effects that this does not apply to are the histamine-release related effects – as once methadone stops entering and rupturing mast cells there is no longer excess histamine being released.

In long-term use blood concentrations are maintained by release of methadone from stores in body tissues. Therefore the withdrawal syndrome associated with methadone may not occur for 1–2 days after the dose has been lowered/stopped.

People completing in-patient detoxification are likely to experience significant withdrawal symptoms for at least 10 days after their last dose of methadone. Severity of withdrawal is affected by patients' anxiety levels, so informing patients about how their symptoms are likely to vary over time can help reduce this.

Withdrawal symptoms
During methadone treatment (or any long-term opiate use) the activity of the neurones that respond to noradrenaline is reduced. If the opiates are removed there is apparently a surge of activity in the neurones resulting in a rise in the levels of noradrenaline.

It is this physiological process together with raised anxiety levels which are largely responsible for the classic opiate withdrawal characteristics listed below:
- Weakness
- Yawning, sneezing
- Sweating
- High temperature but feeling cold
- Tremors
- Goose bumps
- Insomnia
- Irritability, aggression
- Muscle spasm and jerking (especially at night)
- Diarrhoea
- Nausea, vomiting
- Loss of appetite.

The cause of deep aches that people experience as 'painful bones' in their limbs and lower back is not known.

Reduced blood levels caused by weight gain
Dose reduction is not the only cause of withdrawal symptoms: weight gain is another possible cause of reduced methadone levels.

Methadone is fat soluble. It is stored in fats around the body. If a client's weight changes rapidly there will be simultaneous changes in the blood concentration of methadone. If the fat content of the body rises more methadone will be stored so less is active in the bloodstream. If the fat content falls methadone will be released from stores and become active.

Substantial weight changes may merit proportional dose changes in people who are receiving methadone maintenance treatment, and may need to be taken into account at the start of treatment when the initial dose is being calculated.

Drug interactions

Drug	Degree of interaction	Effect	Mechanism
Alcohol[55]		Increased sedation	Additive CNS depression
Barbiturates[75]	Moderate	Reduced methadone levels, raised sedation	Raised hepatic metabolism, additive CNS depression
Benzodiazepines[76]		Enhanced sedative effect	Additive CNS depression
Buprenorphine[75]		Antagonist effect	Can only be used safely in low-dose (20mg or less daily) methadone treatment
Carbamazepine[75]	Moderate	Reduced methadone levels	Raised hepatic metabolism; methadone may need BD dosing regime
Chloral hydrate		Increased sedation	Additive CNS depression
Chlormethiazole[76]		Increased sedation	Additive CNS depression
Cimetidine[55]	Moderate	Possible increase in methadone levels	Inhibits hepatic enzymes involved in methadone metabolism
Cisapride[76] Domperidone[76] Metoclopramide[76]		Morphine has an increased rate of onset of action and increased sedative effect when used with these drugs[69]	Unknown
Cyclizine[55]	Severe	Injection with opiates causing hallucinations reported	Unknown
Codeine[55]		Enhanced sedative effect	Additive CNS depression
Desipramine[75]	Moderate	Raised desipramine levels (x2)	Unknown – interaction not seen with other tricyclic antidepressants

Drug	Degree of Interaction	Effect	Mechanism
Dextropropoxyphene[55]		Enhanced sedative effect	Additive CNS depression
Disulfiram (Antabuse)	Dependant on methadone formulation	Full 'therapeutic' alcohol adverse reaction	Some methadone preparations contain alcohol
MAOI antidepressants including moclobemide and selegiline[76]	Severe with pethidine, although rare with methadone concurrent use should be avoided	CNS excitation – delirium, hyperpyrexia, convulsions or respiratory depression	Unknown
Naltrexone	Severe	Reverses the effects of methadone in overdose (long acting)	Opiate antagonist, works by competing for opiate receptors
Naloxone[55]	Severe	Reverses the effects of methadone in overdose (short acting)	Opiate antagonist, works by competing for opiate receptors
Phenobarbitone[75]	Moderate	Reduced methadone levels	Raised hepatic (liver) metabolism – see carbamazepine
Phenytoin[55]	Moderate	Reduced methadone levels: withdrawal symptoms	Raised hepatic (liver) metabolism – see carbamazepine
Rifampicin[55]	Severe	Reduced methadone levels: withdrawal symptoms	Raised hepatic (liver) metabolism
Tricyclic antidepressants e.g. amitriptyline	Moderate	Increased sedation	Unkown
Urine acidifiers[55] e.g. ammonium chloride		Reduced methadone levels	Raised urinary excretion
Urine alkalinisers[55] e.g. sodium bicarbonate	Moderate	Raised methadone levels	Reduced urinary excretion
Zidovudine[54]		Raised levels of zidovudine possible	Unknown
Zopiclone[54]		Increased sedation	Additive CNS depression

Medical conditions and methadone

As with all opiates methadone causes no damage to any of the major organs. Prolonged use will not cause any direct physical damage other than tooth decay.

Asthma

The action of opiates in releasing histamine (which is a key factor in triggering an asthma attack) means that, in theory, methadone could worsen a pre-existing asthma condition.

This potential risk needs to be weighed against the:

- Stabilising benefits of methadone prescribing which, in reducing stress, may improve the health of someone with asthma
- Effect illicit heroin (with its high peak doses) had on the individual's asthma
- Fact that smoked heroin causes direct irritation of the airways.

Diabetes

Methadone mixture may contain glucose and this can interfere with the control of diabetes. For those clients with diabetes, pharmacists can be asked to dispense a sugar-free preparation.

Epilepsy

Methadone has no anti-convulsant properties, even at high doses.

Other opiates can cause convulsions at very high doses and it is therefore possible that methadone could do the same. If there is a risk of exacerbating existing epilepsy (and there is no evidence that there is) methadone treatment may still improve contact with services, compliance with anti-convulsant therapy as well as making dosage more predictable, and therefore safer, than heroin.

It is important to check which anti-convulsant therapy any client who is epileptic is receiving because carbamazepine and phenytoin interact with methadone (see drug interactions chart above).

Liver disease

Overall, Moore et al[77] considered that liver damage does not unduly disrupt methadone metabolism. A study by Novick et al[78] of people with chronic liver disease on long-term methadone maintenance found that dose need not be altered although they suggest that abrupt changes in liver function might require substantial dose adjustments.

However, if a client had extensive and serious liver damage methadone maintenance treatment would, because of the extra strain placed on the organ, be expected to precipitate a condition called porto-systemic encephalopathy.[55] This is a toxic confusional state caused by the liver failing to metabolise a number of products. This may be temporary and reversable or can result in permanent brain damage.

Therefore, as a precaution, when there may be impaired liver function following hepatitis B or C infection or prolonged alcohol use, methadone dose must be monitored carefully. Particular care must be taken whenever doses of over 50mg are prescribed as there have been a number of overdose deaths reported in the first 2–6 days of treatment and it has been suggested that liver function tests prior to treatment may reduce the risk of overdose.[69]

Pain

Methadone is an analgesic (pain killer) and will therefore mask pain in people who are taking it. The analgesic effect of methadone may fluctuate as the duration of analgesic effect from each dose may well be shorter than its effect in terms of preventing withdrawal symptoms. This could cause pain to break through in the hours before taking the next dose.

Because the disease process may be more advanced than usual before a methadone-using client feels any pain, workers need to be alert to reports of pain. If appropriate they should be investigated promptly in case there is a treatable cause.

It is quite common for opiate users to experience pain if their methadone dose is reduced. This pain may be associated with withdrawal but other causes must be excluded as it may be pain previously masked by high opiate levels.

If not treated, pain may trigger relapse at a later stage, as many opiate users will self-medicate to relieve the discomfort.

If tolerance to opiates is a problem the use of non-opiate analgesia such as aspirin, paracetamol or Non-Steroidal Anti-Inflammatory (NSAIDs) such as ibuprofen may reduce the pain. However it is often difficult to get opiate users – who may have high expectations of analgesics – to accept other treatments.

summary

■ Methadone is a relatively simple, synthetic compound that has similar effects to natural opiates.

■ It acts on many sites in the body causing a complex range of reactions.

■ Methadone is notable for its lack of long-term side effects in comparison to many prescribed drugs.

■ People become tolerant to some effects of methadone, albeit usually very slowly.

■ Tolerance to constipation and pin-point pupils (miosis) is rare.

■ Withdrawal symptoms from methadone are mainly caused by the body reacting to the absence of opiates in the peripheral nervous system.

■ Methadone does not cause congenital abnormality in babies.

■ Methadone is absorbed into, and stored in, a number of sites in the body from where it is gradually released into the bloodstream.

■ Methadone interacts with a number of drugs and a few medical conditions.

■ Methadone overdose is a serious medical emergency requiring urgent response.

■ In treating methadone overdose it must be borne in mind that it is a long-acting compound.

section 5

Methadone

and the law

The supply and possession of methadone   **66**

Writing a methadone prescription   **67**

Which prescription pad?   **67**

Handwriting exemptions   **67**

Dispensing and collection of methadone   **68**

Methadone in hospitals   **69**

Notification to the Home Office   **70**

The 'registered addict'   **70**

Driving   **70**

The Home Office Drugs Inspectorate   **71**

Patients going abroad   **72**

Summary   **73**

65

Introduction

There are two main statutes that regulate the availability of drugs in the UK. The Medicines Act 1968 governs the manufacture and supply of medicinal products of all kinds, and its enforcement rarely affects the general public. It divides drugs into three catagories:

- Prescription-only medicines
- Pharmacy medicines
- General sales list.

Methadone is a prescription-only medicine.

The second of the two statutes is the Misuse of Drugs Act 1971. One of its main functions is to prevent the unauthorised use of certain substances.

Drugs subject to this act are known as controlled drugs. Methadone is a controlled drug.

These two statutes cover many aspects of the production, prescribing, possession, supply, administration and disposal of methadone.

It is important that workers in contact with people using methadone are aware of the legal constraints on, and implications for, themselves and their clients.

The supply and possession of methadone

The manufacture of methadone and the law controlling it is covered in Section 3: Methadone manufacture and the preparations available.

Who can supply and prescribe methadone?

The prescribing of controlled drugs is limited to members of the medical professions. The system of specially licensing doctors to prescribe certain drugs to addicts covers diamorphine (heroin), cocaine and dipipanone (the analgesic ingredient of Diconal) but does not (and never has) extended to methadone.

Registered medical practitioners can prescribe methadone as treatment for pain relief or treatment of addiction.

The only exceptions to the above are doctors who have had their licence to prescribe controlled drugs revoked by the Home Secretary. Pharmacists can check whether or not a doctor has been prohibited from prescribing controlled drugs by telephoning the Home Office on:
- **0171 273 3302**

The prescription of all controlled drugs other than in the course of legitimate treatment is regarded as serious misconduct by the General Medical Council.[79]

Anyone found guilty of illegally supplying methadone to others (including clients who sell or give away their medication) can receive severe penalties under the Misuse of Drugs Act because methadone is a Class A drug.

Possession of methadone

The legal posession of methadone is restricted to:
- Licenced manufacturers
- Medical practitioners
- Nurses or another person dispensing under the direction of a doctor
- Pharmacists
- Someone who has been legally prescribed methadone
- Someone who has found it and is proceeding to a police station.

It is a crime for methadone to be supplied (sold, given, etc.) by anyone who is not authorised by law to do so and it is a crime to be in unauthorised possession of methadone.

Writing a methadone prescription

Controlled drugs should not be prescribed on a repeat prescription basis.

The prescription of methadone is carefully controlled. Only prescriptions which are legally written can be legally dispensed.

There is an example of how to write a methadone prescription on page 160.

The following strict requirements apply to prescriptions for methadone:
■ The prescriber must sign and date the prescription (a date stamp is legal, a computer-generated date is not legal)
■ The prescription must be written in indelible ink
■ Unless it is an NHS or a local health authority prescription it must have the prescriber's address on it (all prescriptions should have the prescriber's telephone number so the pharmacist can ring if there is a problem).

Unless the prescriber has a handwriting exemption (see below) s/he must handwrite the following information on all methadone prescriptions:
■ Name and address of the client
■ Methadone dose, form and strength (e.g. methadone mixture DTF 1mg/mL)
■ Total number of milligrams (or millilitres) of methadone or the number of doses prescribed, in both words and figures.

If the prescription is to be dispensed in instalments the doctor must use the correct pad (see below) and specify:
■ The total quantity prescribed, as above
■ The amount to be supplied per instalment
■ The intervals at which the instalments are to be dispensed (bearing in mind days when the pharmacy may be closed such as weekends and public holidays).

If the prescriber has a handwriting exemption this information can be produced in another way but it must appear on the prescription.

Which prescription pad?

Single collection
In general practice a methadone prescription with a single collection date should be written on a standard white FP10 form. In hospital out-patients an orange FP10 (HP) should be used.

Multiple collections
Multiple collections from a community pharmacy, prescribed by a GP, must be on the blue FP10 (MDA) in England, Wales or Northern Ireland and on a GP10 in Scotland.

Hospital doctors in England, Wales or Northern Ireland should use form FP10(HP)(ad) and in Scotland form HPB(A) should be used.

Handwriting exemptions

The Home Office can give handwriting exemptions to doctors who issue more than 10 controlled drug prescriptions to addicts per week.

This means that prescriptions can be written by key-workers, typed, produced by computer or using a rubber stamp. The doctor need only sign and date them (see above). Prescriptions produced thus must still contain all the information as listed above.

Doctors who need a Home Office handwriting exemption can receive an application form from:

The Licensing Section
Home Office
50 Queen Anne's Gate
London SW1 9AT
Tel: 0171 273 3000 ext. 2446

67

Dispensing and collection of methadone

Methadone is a Schedule 2 controlled drug. Pharmacists are among those who have a general authorisation to procure, possess and supply methadone.

It is a professional requirement for pharmacists to supply methadone in bottles with 'child-resistant' caps. These bottles should be clearly labelled with the quantity of methadone they contain (in case the contents are ingested by accident or someone overdoses). All other labelling requirements for medicines apply as usual.

Receipt of methadone at a pharmacy
Methadone must be received into pharmacy stock by a registered pharmacist. On receipt the quantity supplied should be checked and an entry made in the purchases section of the controlled drugs register. The methadone should then be placed in the controlled drugs cabinet.

Storage of methadone in the pharmacy
Methadone must be stored in a locked safe, cabinet or 'room which is so constructed and maintained as to prevent unauthorised access'. When methadone is removed from storage it must remain under the direct personal supervision of a pharmacist.

Supply of methadone from a pharmacy
All methadone supplies must be recorded on dispensing in accordance with the Misuse of Drugs Act legislation.

For a controlled drug to be supplied to an individual they must be in possession of a prescription.

Before dispensing the pharmacist has to be satisfied that the:
- Prescription is written correctly (see above)
- Prescriber's address as written on the prescription is within the UK
- Prescriber's signature is known to the pharmacist or has been checked and found to be legitimate
- Date of supply is after the date specified on the prescription
- Date of supply is within 13 weeks of the date on the prescription.

The prescription must be dated at the time of dispensing. It must then be retained by the pharmacist for 2 years (except in the case of NHS and LHA prescriptions).[30]

Collecting methadone
On-site/in-patient administration of methadone and take-out methadone dispensing can be done only in accordance with an individual medical prescription. Methadone prescribed for an individual should only be supplied to that person.

Clients who are unable to attend to collect their own methadone and who wish another person to collect the dose/s on their behalf should provide proof that this is their intention. The same is true for collecting the paper prescription from the prescribing service.

These safeguards help protect the confidentiality of the client regarding their treatment, and prevent theft by people posing as friends and collecting methadone which they have no intention of passing on to the person to whom it belongs.

Collection in instalments
Prescriptions to be supplied in instalments must be dispensed in accordance with directions. The first instalment must be dispensed within 13 weeks of prescribing. The pharmacist must date the prescription at the time of each dispensation, and make the appropriate entry in the controlled drugs register.

The NHS provides special prescription forms for daily supplies of methadone to be dispensed to drug users: see above.

Requests for missed or late collections

Clients who collect their methadone from a community pharmacist sometimes come in a day early or a day late for their methadone. Strictly speaking they should receive no methadone. In practice some pharmacists will dispense a day late, omitting the dose for the day they did not collect, although this is not in accordance with the law.

However requests to collect methadone early (whatever the reason) should be referred back to the drug service or prescribing doctor. Such requests are often an indication that either things are not going well and the client is using more than the prescribed daily dose of methadone and is able to miss doses because they are using other substances, or that the pick-up days are unsuitable because of work or other committments.

Methadone in hospitals

Destruction of methadone at a ward or clinic

Methadone stocks not required on the ward can be returned to the pharmacy for destruction. A methadone dose specifically prepared for a patient to take home should also be returned to the pharmacy and destroyed if not collected by the patient.

Destruction of methadone at the pharmacy

Any methadone which is recorded as part of the pharmacy stock and needs to be destroyed (for instance if it has passed its expiry date or if there is no longer a need to stock methadone), must be done so only in the presence of an 'authorised person'.

However if methadone that has been dispensed is returned to the pharmacy it can be destroyed by a pharmacist without the presence of an authorised person, and should not be re-entered into the pharmacy stock.

Notification to the Home Office

When and whom doctors should notify

The Misuse of Drugs Act 1973 requires doctors to notify the Chief Medical Officer at the Home Office within 7 days if they attend a patient who they consider to be, or have reasonable grounds to suspect is, addicted to any of the controlled drugs listed below:

- Cocaine
- Palfium
- Diamorphine (heroin)
- Dipipanone (Diconal)
- Hydrocodone
- Hydromorphone
- Levorphanol
- Methadone
- Morphine
- Opium
- Oxycodone
- Pethidine
- Phenazocine
- Piritamide.

This includes patients who:
- Are temporary residents
- Are referred by another doctor/service
- Are known to be in receipt of treatment from another doctor
- Have recently been in receipt of treatment from another doctor
- Are known to have been recently notified to the Home Office
- The doctor decides not to treat.

What doctors should notify

There are forms available from your local FHSA/Health Commission but notifications can be made by letter and should contain the following information about the patient:
- Name
- Address
- Gender
- Date of birth
- NHS number (if known)
- Date of attendance
- Drugs concerned
- Whether or not the patient injects
- What, if anything, was prescribed.

They should be sent to:

The Drugs Branch
Home Office
50 Queen Anne's Gate
London SW1 9AT

Confidentiality

The information is confidentially stored on the Addicts Index which is only used by doctors to verify the history given by new patients and for research purposes.

Using the Addicts Index

Doctors can check the medical history of patients who present to them for treatment of a drug problem during office hours by phoning the Addicts Index direct on: **0171 273 2213.**

Outside office hours an answering machine will take messages. Callers will be phoned back and given details of doctors who had previously notified the patient.

The 'registered addict'

The status of having been notified to the Home Office is often termed as being a 'registered addict', but there is, in fact, no such status.

Being notified to the Addicts Index is often much overrated or feared by drug users. In fact notification confers no rights to treatment nor loss of civil liberties and is simply a system to prevent multiple prescribing, to facilitate research and to inform funding decisions. There has never been a confirmed case of information from the register being passed to the police, visa authorities or anyone other than doctors enquiring about their patients.

Informing the users of this may help reduce the anxiety associated with notification.

The police may find out that people are being treated with methadone but this will be via the Pharmacy Inspecting Officer system – see below.

Regional databases

Alongside the notification system there is also the regional database system, which exists in most areas. This is a non-compulsory system which counts the number of drug users presenting to services and gives a brief outline of their problems. It is used for gathering statistical information and informing purchasing decisions. This information is also stored confidentially and personal information is not passed to any third party.

Driving

Driving licence

The Road Traffic Act requires holders of, or applicants for, a driving licence to inform the Driver Vehicle Licensing Authority (DVLA) of '...any disability likely to affect safe driving'. DVLA considers drug use, including the use of prescribed drugs, to be a 'disability' in this context.

This responsibility lies with the holder or applicant, not the prescribing doctor or drug service.

DVLA will not issue a group 2 (HGV/PSV) licence to anyone receiving methadone treatment.

If a client with a group 1 driving licence informs DVLA that they are receiving an oral methadone prescription they are then required to have a short (free) independent medical examination. This includes a urine screen for drugs. If there are only methadone metabolites in the urine a licence is normally issued for one year. They will be called back for another medical every year until 3 years after methadone treatment has finished.

If a client informs DVLA that they are receiving injectable methadone on prescription, the licence may be withdrawn, although a letter from a consultant psychiatrist confirming that the client experiences low levels of sedation can result in a decision to treat the prescription of injectable methadone in the same way as oral methadone.

On re-application the client will have to undergo a medical including a urine screen for drugs. They will be called back for another medical every year until 3 years after methadone treatment has finished.

If the urine screen carried out for the DVLA medical shows positive for cannabis they will withdraw the licence for 6 months. If it shows positive for any other drug they will withdraw the licence for 12 months. There will be another medical on re-application and every year for the first 3 years after the licence has been returned.

Driving under the influence of methadone

It is also an offence to be in charge of a vehicle if 'unfit to drive through drink or drugs'. A client taking methadone would not automatically be considered by the courts to be unfit to drive and the onus of proof is on the prosecution to prove that s/he was unfit to drive because of the methadone.

insurance companies may also consider a methadone prescription as an additional risk about which they should have been informed, and may contest claims from drivers who are discovered to have been receiving prescribed methadone at the time of an accident.

Whether or not practitioners should take the step of breaching confidence and informing DVLA without their client's consent, if they are concerned about a client's ability to drive or if the client is driving passenger or heavy goods vehicles, is a complex ethical issue.

Guidance should be sought from professional bodies in terms of professional responsibility and from the practitioner's line manager for guidance in terms of their employment. The correct course of action will depend on the balance of exercising the duty of care for the client and the community – weighing the relative risks of accident and injury with the benefits in terms of client and community safety of continued client contact.

In cases where ability to drive under the influence of methadone is an issue the problem of confidentiality can be easily avoided by encouraging the client to either contact DVLA themselves or giving the practitioner permission to do so.

The Home Office Drugs Inspectorate

The primary function of the Inspectorate – together with the Licensing Section – is to control the manufacture and distribution of controlled drugs. The controls and the drugs to which they apply are laid down in the Misuse of Drugs Act 1971 and dependant regulations.

The Inspectorate:
■ Makes recommendations on the suitability of applicants for licences to manufacture and store controlled drugs
■ Determines the precautions which must be taken for safe custody of controlled drugs in the possession of a licensee
■ Inspects security, documentation and record keeping
■ Investigates irresponsible prescribing of controlled drugs by doctors.

Irresponsible prescribing may lead to a doctor's prescribing practice being referred to a Misuse of Drugs Tribunal which can recommend to the Home Secretary that he use his power to ban the doctor from prescribing controlled drugs. Irresponsible prescribing usually constitutes prescribing high doses of inappropriate drugs to large numbers of people despite cautioning from the Drugs Inspectorate, and not the legitimate prescription of methadone, with appropriate support, to heroin users.

In addition to its inspectorial and investigative functions the Inspectorate also acts as the agency within the Home Office which liaises between central government and other bodies at a regional and local level concerned with drug misuse.

Pharmacy inspecting officers

Retail chemists' controlled drugs registers are inspected by the police for the Home Office Drugs Inspectorate. The person who does this has the title of the 'Chemists Inspecting Officer'. It is as a result of this that cases of irresponsible prescribing would normally come to light.

However as the Chemists Inspecting Officers usually work as part of the drug squad and have no obligation to keep the information they have gained confidential, it is through this route that local police forces often find out that people have methadone prescriptions.

Patients going abroad

If a client is travelling abroad and is carrying a supply of methadone they will require a Home Office licence if they are taking more than 15 days' supply or 500 mg of methadone.

Export licences are issued by:

**The Drugs Licensing Section
Home Office
Room 230
50 Queen Anne's Gate
London SW1H 9AT**

There is no standard application form. Application must be made by the person who wants to take the methadone out of the country.

They should write to the Home Office at the address above, enclosing a letter from their prescribing doctor, giving the following details:
- Name and address
- Quantities of drugs to be carried
- Strength and form in which the drugs will be dispensed
- Date of travel from the United Kingdom
- Date of return.

The Licence is required under the Misuse of Drugs Act to facilitate passage through UK Customs Control. However, clients should be aware that it has no legal status outside the UK. To find out whether methadone can be taken into the country/countries the client is visiting they should contact the relevant Embassy or Consulate well before departure.

If a client is planning to go abroad for an extended period and wishes to take a supply of methadone it may be possible to arrange for a clinic to prescribe in the country concerned. The Embassy or Consulate may be able to advise if this is possible and give the names of clinics.

A Home Office licence is not necessary for amounts under 500mg provided the client is not carrying more than 14 days' supply, although it is advisable to carry a 'to whom it may concern' letter from the prescribing doctor confirming that the client is in possession of the methadone for legitimate medical purposes.

summary

■ All doctors can write a prescription for methadone which is prescribed in the same way as all other controlled drugs.

■ Doctors must notify the Home Office Drugs Branch if they attend anyone who they believe to be addicted to heroin, methadone or any one of a number of other drugs – even if they know that the patient has already been notified.

■ The Home Office Drugs Inspectorate receive reports from Chemist Inspecting Officers about pharmacy controlled drugs registers.

■ Chemist Inspecting Officers usually work as part of the drug squad and they may pass information about who has a methadone prescription to their colleagues.

■ Clients taking large quantities of methadone abroad are required to apply for an export licence.

section 6

Assessment

Assessment length and setting	**76**
Setting the scene	**77**
Methadone assessment checklist	**79**
Going through the assessment checklist	**82**
General information	**82**
Drug-using history	**82**
Life history	**85**
Current situation	**86**
Objective support for your assessment	**87**
Summary	**88**

Introduction

Assessment of opiate use is not an exact science. The outcome of an assessment will depend on the interpretation by the assessor of the:
- Client's description of their feelings
- History the client gives
- The amount, type, route of administration and frequency of drugs the client says they are using
- Objective signs of use (injection marks, urinalysis etc.)
- Signs of intoxication/withdrawal.

The assessment will be affected by:
- Who is assessing
- The type of agency in which the assessment is taking place
- The services available
- The degree of specialist knowledge the assessor has.

The objectives of an assessment for the suitability of methadone treatment are the same whatever the setting, namely to determine:
- Is the person an opiate user?
- Have they been previously notified to the Home Office?
- Are they already receiving methadone treatment from another prescriber?
- Is methadone an appropriate treatment?

and to give the client an understanding of:
- The treatment options available
- The difference between the experience of heroin and methadone.

Subsequent sections look at the issues of determining the length of treatment and starting methadone dose.

The headings below cover the core components of a good initial assessment (see checklist below) and describe some of the tools that can be used to help decide on treatment goals and, later, to measure their effectiveness.

Assessment length and setting

People who are requesting help with their opiate problems are usually assessed either:
- In the community
- As a day patient of a drug service or hospital unit
- As a hospital/drug unit in-patient over a few days.

Community assessments

The majority of assessments are done in the community. Most community assessments are done over one or more one-hour sessions with the client. They do not usually require the client to be observed withdrawing from opiates or be supervised taking a 'test dose' of methadone.

Day patient and in-patient assessments

In-patient and day assessments are more expensive and require specialist staff but they can be more objective because they give the opportunity for the client to be assessed:
- Very closely
- Over a long period of time
- By a multidisciplinary team
- Experiencing withdrawal symptoms
- Following the administration of methadone.

They also allow more time to develop a therapeutic relationship, give health education information and to discuss issues such as injecting practice and HIV.

This type of assessment may be indicated when:
- There is some doubt about the level of opiate use
- The person is requesting a high dose of methadone
- There are complicating factors such as heavy poly drug use or medical problems.

Setting the scene

It is important to give the client an understanding of the purpose of the assessment process right from the outset. Most initial community assessments are one hour long.

It is important that the client knows at the start:
- How long the interview is likely to last
- How it will be structured
- The purpose of any notes you take
- Your policies on confidentiality
- What the treatment options might be.

This will help the client disclose the information you need to make the assessment and will prevent them from having unrealistic expectations of what you are able to do at the end of the assessment.

Why are you doing the assessment?
Explain that the key functions of the assessment are to get:
- A clear picture of the problems besetting the user

and to ensure that your response:
- Is appropriate/helpful
- Will not make them dependent on a larger dose of methadone than necessary.

Will I get a methadone prescription?
This is usually the client's overriding concern and it may manifest itself as anxiety, anger or behaviours such as threatening to commit suicide or break the law to obtain supplies, etc. Sometimes clients will say that if they do not get a prescription it will be the worker's/doctor's responsibility if they go out and overdose or break into a pharmacy etc. to obtain supplies. However the drug use and associated behaviour is the responsibility of the client – not you. Clarity about the framework within which you are both working will minimise these behaviours because it will be clear that they will not increase the likelihood of the outcome the client wants. It is useful to tell the client that it is your

intention to help them as best you can, and that if methadone is to be prescribed you would want it to be enough so that it will be of some help to them. If you are not the prescriber it is important to explain what your relationship with the prescriber is and what role your assessment plays in the prescribing decision.

A client who knows that you are willing to prescribe or arrange a methadone prescription, if you think it is the right thing to do, is much more likely to relax and co-operate. It is therefore important to advise the client of the timescale of response to a request for prescribing.

Never allow yourself to be pressurised into a course of action you are unhappy about and make it clear that you retain the right to make a clinical judgement to refuse to commence or to withdraw treatment if there is evidence that it is not therapeutic.

Honesty
Try to reassure the client that you are not going to halve all their reports of their recent drug use so there is no need for them to double everything. This may come as a big surprise and, of course, they may not entirely believe you so exaggeration may still be a feature of the history you are given.

It is still important to try and establish an honest, trusting relationship with the client while looking at a range of indicators and asking questions about recent drug use in a number of ways.

Confidentiality
Clients need to know that you do not have a hot-line to the local police station, their parents, etc. If people are going to give informed consent to the passing on of personal information they need to know exactly what confidentiality means to you and your agency.

It is a good idea to do this at both the beginning and the end of the interview – at the beginning in broad terms and at the end you can discuss in detail what information needs to be passed on, to whom and how that is going to be done.

There is further discussion about confidentiality in Section 10: Practical issues in methadone prescribing.

Using a standard assessment format
Each agency should have its own written assessment format. This allows you to make sure that:
■ You do not miss anything
■ All clients get the same assessment, regardless of who carries it out
■ You have a written record of what you did and why you did it.

The checklist below can be used as a basis for an assessment.

The Home Office and/or local database notification forms can be used to give a swift documented record of an individual's current drug use – but they are no substitute for a prepared assessment process and format.

A number of assessment and diagnosis tools have been developed over the years. These include:
■ Leeds Dependence Questionnaire[81]
■ The Substance Abuse Assessment Questionnaire[82]
■ The Severity of Opiate Dependence Questionnaire (SODQ)[83]
■ The Diagnostic and Statistical Manual of the American Psychiatric Association, 4th edition.[84]

These tools, when skilfully applied, provide very accurate, standardised formats for assessing the level of dependence. They are not all very worker or client 'friendly'. Unless workers are familiar with the format the gains made in having standard information are lost in a more impersonal interaction. However some, such as the Leeds Dependence Questionnaire, are quick, easy and reliable tools.

Methadone assessment checklist

General information

Assessor:

Assessment date:

Urine specimen taken for drug screen: YES/NO

Name:

Date of birth:

Age:

Address:

79

Telephone number:
(and correspondence address/telephone number if different)

General practitioner:

Who referred the client to your agency:

Other agencies involved with the client, e.g. social services, probation, etc:

Current legal situation – outstanding prosecutions, etc:

Methadone assessment checklist

Drug-using history

Current drug(s) used:

Amount(s) currently used:

Primary drug:

Other drugs:

Alcohol use – units per day and week:

Pattern of use:

History of injecting:

Age of first use:

Drug used:

History and pattern:

Periods of abstinence/causes of relapse:

Methadone sssessment checklist

Personal history

Life history:

Employment history:

Mental health history:

Physical health history:

Current situation

Events leading to referral:

Motivation to attend:

Current family situation:

Client's summary of problems:

Client's hypothesis of reasons for drug/alcohol use and service/help requested:

Overall impression:

Conclusion:

Going through the assessment checklist

An assessment of someone requesting a methadone prescription should cover the following areas:
■ General information
■ Drug-using history
■ Life history
■ Current physical, social and psychological situations
■ Reasons for seeking help
■ Conclusions.

This section goes through the assessment checklist above outlining the information you need and how it can be gathered under the headings, which are not just straightforward questions.

There may appear to be a lot of questions. This is partly because drug users are not always forthcoming about all aspects of their life. This is not surprising – many have had unfortunate experiences at the hands of health and other helping professionals. So if you do not ask you may not find out – until it is too late!

General information

Clients will often present with high levels of anxiety. The taking of basic information can help relax and engage them in the assessment process.

Other agencies involved

Knowledge of which other agencies are involved can both help you understand the complexity of the client's problems and plan with the client what liaison, if any, you are going to have with those agencies.

Current legal situation

Fear of a custodial sentence is often a motivator for seeking help, which needs to be identified early on in the care plan as it can dictate the time frame within which you are working. It is therefore important to get details of any:
■ Charges faced
■ Pending court cases
■ Probation orders.

Drug-using history

Current drug(s) used

Opiate users often use a combination of other drugs alongside their heroin use. They may not consider their benzodiazepine use significant or relevant enough to disclose unless asked directly about it. It is also important to ask if they are receiving any other prescribed medication.

Primary drug used

This is important, particularly in the case of opiate use/assessment for methadone prescribing. Obviously if you are thinking of methadone prescribing you need to be sure that it is the right thing to do. There is little point in giving methadone to someone who is:
■ Not dependent on opiates
■ Using mainly non-opiate drugs such as amphetamine, cocaine or alcohol.

Establishing current levels of opiate use

Current opiate use is a key area to assess correctly because if a decision is taken to prescribe methadone the dose will, to a large extent, be determined by the amount of opiates the client is thought to be taking. This is discussed further in Section 9: Getting the starting dose right.

In a system that relies largely on judgements based upon what people say, there are several factors that can complicate the assessment.

Clients often:

■ Presume that decisions on the amount of methadone they receive will be based on their current opiate consumption

■ Think their account will be believed to be exaggerated and therefore exaggerate accordingly to compensate

■ Represent current levels of use according to the amount they use on 'good' days.

For this reason the current levels of opiate use need to be returned to several times, and in several ways, during the course of the assessment. A model for doing this in 4 'phases' during the assessment is outlined below.

During the course of the assessment – as the client becomes more relaxed – go through the following points in groups such as the ones suggested below. In these lists the word heroin can be substituted with the person's opiate(s) of choice.

Phase 1

■ How much heroin do you take a day?
■ How much did you take yesterday?
■ How much, on average, do you take in a week?
■ How much have you had so far today?

Phase 2

■ How many days a week do you take heroin?
■ How do you feel after you've taken heroin?
■ How long after you've taken some does it take before you feel rough again?
■ What withdrawal symptoms are you experiencing now?
■ What do the withdrawals feel like?

Phase 3

■ How much do you buy at a time?
■ How much do you pay per gram?
■ How much is your habit costing you a day?
■ How much did you take on the day you had most last week?
■ How many days in the last week did you have any opiates?

Phase 4

■ How much do you spend a week on heroin?
■ How much heroin can you get by with on your worst days?
■ How often do you score in a day?
■ When was the last time you had an opiate free day?
■ Have there been times when you have stopped all opiate use for more than 3 days?

It will be difficult for someone who is not an opiate user to answer all the above questions consistently and accurately. If your client is an opiate user the pattern of their answers will usually give you a good idea of the level of their opiate use because it is difficult without preparation to consistently lie across such a broad range of questions.

Alcohol use

A minority of people presenting for methadone treatment have significant alcohol problems. For some the main attraction of methadone is its ability to potentiate the action of alcohol.

Where this may be the case treatment aims need to be clearly specified.

The interplay between opiate and alcohol use needs to be clearly understood by both the worker and client – and disproportionate attention to opiates (and inappropriate methadone prescribing) need to be avoided.

For many opiate users the process of understanding their alcohol use in terms of units consumed and potential harm is a useful exercise.

Pattern of drug use

As well as how much the person is taking you also need a broader picture of their current pattern of drug use.

Is the drug use:
- Experimental: being tried out
- Recreational: used intermittently and with some control
- Compulsive: dependent daily use with physical and psychological dependence and little perceived control over the use?

Most people who present are in the latter category and methadone treatment is unlikely to be of value for people in the former groups.

Is the heroin:
- Smoked
- Injected
- or both?

Do they take heroin:
- With friends
- At the dealers
- Alone
- Don't care as long as they've got some?

How much at a time?
- Quantities of the drug used at each use
- How long is each drug-using episode
- How long does a purchase last
- Can they save some for the morning?

History of injecting
Injecting is the riskiest way of introducing a drug into the body. It by-passes the body's natural defences by putting the substance straight into the bloodstream. People who inject are taking more risks than people who do not, the risks being infection, overdose and transmission of disease to or from themselves.

The risks are not only concerned with sharing syringes, and a supplement to any assessment for methadone prescribing should be a detailed assessment of injecting practices and an opportunity for the user to discuss this issue in detail.

An inspection of all injection sites should be carried out both to verify that they exist and to check for infection and other complications of injecting.

Drug-taking history
It is important to get a perspective of the current opiate use in terms of the person's drug-taking history.

Ask about any other drugs they have taken, starting with their first ever drug use. Chart each drug with the following details:
- Age of first use
- Pattern of use from then on
- Reasons why it was first taken
- Reasons why they continued to use it
- How its use related to other drugs used
- When (if) its use was stopped and why.

If the client has had times free from each drug ask:
- How long were these periods?
- What symptoms of withdrawal did you experience?
- Did you replace the drug with anything else?
- What started you using it again?

A history of drug-free times and the causes of relapse can be a great help in planning care and strategies for the future.

A pattern of switching dependence from one drug to another (particularly alcohol and benzodiazepines) is likely to reduce the chances of methadone prescribing being an effective intervention in the medium or long term if the client is likely to continue with this pattern.

Life history

It is important that methadone treatment is seen in the context of wider psycho-social help. The taking of a comprehensive history demonstrates that dealing with issues arising from the past may be part of the treatment.

Clearly the amount and quality of information gathered when taking the life history will be determined by the state of mind of the client and the quality of the relationship that can be built in the first session. If taking a full history is not appropriate or possible in the first session then it is useful to return to it at a later date.

As with any counselling or psychiatric assessment, open questioning which will allow the client to tell you about their background is important.
Areas covered would normally include:
- Early childhood
- Parental relationships
- Siblings
- Moves and schooling
- Abuse (childhood and/or recent)
- Relationships
- Marriage
- Employment/unemployment

and the other areas described below.

The criminal 'justice' system
A significant minority of people who are opiate dependent will have a history of court appearances. These range from cautions for possession, convictions for supply through to major prison sentences for drugs offences or related crimes such as:
- Theft
- Burglary
- Violent offences (these may have implications for case management).

Taking a history of offences, prosecutions and sentences may also provide a useful opportunity to assess the importance of problem drinking as offences committed under the influence of alcohol suggest that this may be a potential problem area.

Mental health
Any history of depression, psychosis or other mental health problems is of importance as these indicate areas in which future problems may arise.

Also check for previous admissions to psychiatric hospitals or out-patient clinics, suicide attempts and overdoses. See also section 11: Prescribing for groups with special needs.

Physical health
Many opiate users have low incomes, lead unhealthy lifestyles and have little contact with health care services. Health difficulties they encounter may be directly related to the drugs themselves or may be a consequence of their lifestyle.

It is important to ask about past and present health problems and be aware of possible future ones during the assessment. Usually a general question about health will be enough to prompt the client, but in particular be alert for the following:
- HIV/AIDS – everyone involved in the care of drug users should be familiar with the signs and symptoms of HIV-related illness
- Impaired liver function which may be caused by hepatitis B or C or alcohol use
- Untreated chest infections – common in opiate users as the cough reflex is suppressed by opiates and most are smokers
- Weight loss
- Psychiatric/neurological problems e.g. epilepsy, head injury or psychotic episodes
- Digestion: constipation is common in opiate users
- Localised infections such as abscesses
- Poor dental health
- Pregnancy.

Do not forget that drug users may have the complication of underlying illness or injury masked by the analgesic effects of opiates. Doctors assessing drug users should always include a physical examination.

Current situation

Events leading to referral

There are several topics to cover under this heading that will help you build up a picture of what has brought this person to seek help and what services will best help them address their problems.

Motivation to attend

Determining why someone is seeking help now is a key issue as it will underpin your understanding of what changes they want to make and why, which in turn informs your decision about what treatment aims to pursue.

Current family situation

An understanding of the family and other relationships that affect the user is important in offering appropriate help. Questions such as the following can all help in gaining an understanding of the relationships affecting the client:

■ How has the drug use affected the family?
■ Have there been breakdowns of relationships because of the use?
■ What do the family think about the use?
■ Are they worried or frightened?
■ Do they need help and support in their own right?
■ Can they offer support or assistance?

Child care

Issues around drug-using parents are also covered in Section 11: Prescribing for groups with special needs – Care of people with responsibility for young people.

It is important to ascertain at assessment whether clients have responsibility for the care of any young people, and if so, their ability to discharge that responsibility.

Current social situation

In terms of a social life:
■ Do they have friends who are not in the drug scene or does life revolve around drugs and other drug users?
■ Do they still have a job or prospects of one?
■ Do they have any interests or rewarding activities other than drugs?
■ Are they able to form and sustain relationships?

Answers to these questions will give you a good insight into the importance that the clients place on drugs in their lives and to the support structures they have in place if they are looking at stopping using drugs.

Finances

The financial health of the client is often a key indicator. Many people sell drugs to support their consumption, and many become involved with crime and/or get into debt.

A moderate to heavy UK consumer of illicit heroin using say 1 gram per day may need to generate at least £300 cash per week, or they may obtain drugs by other means, such as working in the sex industry or by exchanging goods for drugs.

The client may have worries and concerns about drug and/or other 'normal' household debts that they need to discuss.

Objective support for your assessment

It is important to arrange, as soon as possible, for a urine sample to be sent to the pathology lab for a drug screen or to use a portable test at the time of assessment.

An opiate-positive urine test in the notes of everyone with a methadone prescription is an essential safeguard for all concerned. Urinalysis is discussed further in Section 10: Practical issues in methadone prescribing.

Liaison with other agencies involved, with the consent of the client, can provide useful corroboration of the history and can help you plan a co-ordinated approach.

Checking injection sites for 'track marks' is good evidence of injecting although some people, through careful injection technique, manage to inject leaving virtually no trace on the skin. A record of the number and extent of injection sites along with a description of the associated bruising and inflammation can be useful in determining the success of treatment.

Observation of the client in withdrawals and post-methadone dose also provides a relatively objective measure of opiate dependence. However many opiate users (especially those who have been using illicit methadone) do not produce text book observable withdrawal symptoms even 18 hours after their last dose.

summary

■ Comprehensive assessment is a key component in effective treatment of opiate users.

■ Methadone is a controlled drug with high dependency potential and a low lethal dose, therefore it should only be prescribed where there is certain knowledge of recent opiate use and where there is a care plan which includes clear treatment goals.

■ If there is any doubt at all in the mind of a prescriber as to the wisdom of prescribing it is important to remember that there is almost certainly more risk in mis-prescribing than in not prescribing.

■ Specialist advice and assessment is usually available to non-specialist services.

section 7

Treatment

aims and

treatment

choices

Motivation and change	**90**
Harm reduction	**92**
Treatment aims	**92**
Is prescribing methadone appropriate?	**93**
Determining optimum treatment duration	**93**
Short-term detoxification	**94**
Long-term detoxification	**95**
Short-term maintenance	**96**
Long-term maintenance	**97**
Treatment setting	**98**
Prescribing injectable methadone	**100**
Diamorphine prescribing	**102**
Summary	**104**

Introduction

Assessment allows us to formulate ideas about what the client needs so we can begin to look at the viability of the treatment options available. The treatment options that can be offered will probably depend largely on what facilities exist in your area as, with the exception of residential rehabilitation, funders are unlikely to buy treatment from outside their area.

Treatment choice must be guided by detailed assessment and clear treatment goals.

This section looks in broad terms at two of the principles underlying methadone prescribing:
- Motivation and change
- Harm reduction.

It then outlines:
- Treatment options that are available
- Criteria for choosing the optimum methadone treatment duration.

Motivation and change

A model of understanding drug-using behaviour and the process of changing it that is used by many clinicians in the field to inform their practice is 'the stages of change' model proposed by Prochaska and DiClimente.[85]

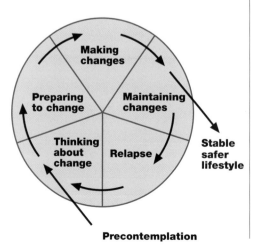

Precontemplation

'Motivational interviewing' is the name given to the use of interventions, designed using this model, to help people achieve change in the component behaviours of their drug dependence and/or abstinence. Many clinicians use other psycho-social and counselling approaches to help clients resolve problems in all areas of their life while using the stages of change model to understand the processes the client is going through in terms of their drug use.

Most people who achieve lasting change in any ingrained behaviour do not achieve it at their first attempt. This is equally true for opiate use; most people who become lastingly opiate free have been through a series of detoxifications and relapses which finally result in a lasting abstinence.

It is possible to learn from each unsuccessful attempt, and to use the lessons learned to achieve better results in the future. The chances of success are higher if someone has been through the process of stopping and starting again than if they are stopping for the first time. For this reason it may be more helpful to view the process as progressing along an upward spiral rather than going round in circles.

Precontemplation: 'Problem, what problem?'

In this stage the drug user has no concerns about their drug use. Other people may have concerns and indeed the drug user may suffer all sorts of problems as a result of the drug use – but not identify drugs as the cause.

This perception can be reinforced by spending a lot of time with other drug users, thus rendering the problems they experience as 'normal' or by rationalising 'everybody takes something' or 'the people with a problem are the ones who are worse than me'.

People in precontemplation often benefit from the opportunity to get their drug use in perspective, to understand which of their problems are drug-related and to understand the reasons why they are using drugs.

If, to improve health or to achieve other goals, we wish to change the drug-using behaviour of a precontemplator, the initial aim is to enable them to weigh up the pros and cons of their drug use and to recognise problems and to attribute them accurately.

Contemplation: 'I'm not happy, but I'm not sure what to do'
People in the contemplation stage are concerned about their drug use but are often not sure what they can do – and may be ambivalent about whether or not they want to do anything. This may result in huge changes in what someone wants to do (and in their behaviour) from day to day.

It is in this stage, as much as in relapse, that contemplators frustrate helpers with urgent requests for help that are then not followed through. People may ask for a detox one day, relapse only a few days into the programme and come back a week later demanding an in-patient detox, but then fail to attend the assessment interview.

At this stage clients will benefit from help in understanding their predicament, coming to a stable decision about what they want, and identifying strategies to achieve it.

Action: 'I'm making changes'
It is at this stage that people implement the strategies and make the changes in their behaviour that they identified while contemplating change.

People spend the least time in action: the strategies either fail and they go back to thinking about change or they move on to maintenance. At this stage they need support, encouragement and help to develop a sense of perspective: it can be an emotionally fragile time.

Maintenance of behaviour change
This is an active state of holding on to the changes made. Complacency is the main enemy of maintenance.

The (ex)drug user may feel as if they have made it and fail to consider ways of holding on to the changes they have made – or look for danger signs. The helping services are often inclined to discharge the people in maintenance and go back to dealing with the more demanding contemplators.

When in maintenance people may benefit from help in identifying things that may go wrong, access to help in dealing with problems before they get out of hand and peer support from other people who are maintaining the same changes.

Relapse
This is a common successor to maintenance. The following cues often precipitate relapse:[86]
Negative mood states:
■ Boredom
■ Depression
■ Anxiety
■ Anger

Social situations:
■ Other people using drugs
■ Offers of drugs
■ Partners relapsing
■ Unexpected problems

Associations:
■ Flu
■ Media mentioning drugs
■ People
■ Places
■ Money.

It can be useful to work with clients to plan strategies for coping with relapse should it occur, but this has to be done carefully to avoid discouraging the client from attempting change.

Relapse need not be an entirely negative event. Indeed since most people who sustain maintenance have relapsed several times on their way, it is an important part of the process. Worker and client should be clear that an attempt to withdraw from drug use which ends in relapse is ultimately worthwhile as a step towards lasting change.

The value of this model is in reminding us that it is too simplistic to think of people as motivated or unmotivated. People are at different stages of motivation for different behaviours. It also puts into perspective (especially when compared to dieting or smoking) the attempts to achieve huge changes such as going from dependent drug use to abstinence.

Harm reduction

Adjuncts or alternatives to methadone treatment

A full menu of services to support methadone treatment would include:
- In-patient detoxification
- In-patient assessment
- Out-patient lofexidine detoxification
- Out-patient dihydrocodeine or buprenorphine treatment
- Prescribing injectable drugs
- Prescribing diamorphine (heroin)
- Breathalysing facilities
- Supervised Antabuse
- HIV testing and counselling
- Mental health services
- Counselling
- Psychotherapy
- Alternative therapies
- Employment advice
- Skills training
- Recreational activities
- Residential rehabilitation
- Supervised naltrexone

Important as all of these can be in supporting and enhancing the outcome of methadone treatment, many of them are, unfortunately, beyond the scope of this briefing and so cannot be described in detail.

Treatment aims

Before 1986 very often the only treatment aim on offer was abstinence. Even today many members of the helping professions are ambivalent about their role in working with drug users and feel (like some ex drug users) that the only 'real' treatment goal is abstinence.

Proponents of harm reduction are aiming at abstinence, as an ultimate goal, for most of their clients. The key to effective treatment is in the time scale that is envisaged before this goal can be reached, and the services that are offered to the drug user in the period before they are ready and/or able to achieve abstinence.

Methadone can be used in a number of ways to help people reduce their drug-related harm and to help them towards abstinence.

Justifiable aims for a methadone prescription would include achieving sustained contact with services that can offer the following:
- Advice and information on HIV and hepatitis
- Safer drug-using advice
- Safer injecting advice
- Counselling
- Support, etc.

and:
- Cessation of injecting
- Significant reduction in illicit drug use
- Reduction of high risk behaviour to acquire/take drugs
- Increased stability in drug use
- Reduced crime
- Improvement of relationships
- Cessation of heroin use
- Cessation of other drug use
- Ability to maintain or gain employment
- Ability to maintain or start a college course
- Reduction in drug use
- Detoxification and abstinence.

Is prescribing methadone appropriate?

Methadone treatment may be justified if the following criteria are met:
■ The client is a non-injector who has been opiate dependent for more than 6 months
■ The client is opiate dependent and injecting opiates

and methadone:
■ Is not going to increase drug-related harm
■ Will help achieve appropriately set short and long-term aims from the list above.

However methadone is not an innocuous treatment and inappropriate methadone prescribing can:
■ Cause fatal overdose
■ Simply increase a person's total drug consumption
■ Increase the drug-related chaos in a person's life
■ Supply the illicit market
■ Demoralise prescribing and other staff
■ Reduce respect for the prescribing agency among both drug users and other helping agencies
■ Reduce the client's motivation and ability to achieve abstinence
■ Create opiate dependence.

Other reasons why someone might ask for a methadone prescription

Treatment of opiate use does not begin and end with methadone. Where people are not using opiates daily, or if they are using very low doses, medical treatments may be of very low priority. Not everyone who presents requesting a methadone prescription is a bona fide opiate dependent looking for help in changing their drug use. Other reasons might include their wanting the following:

■ A 'status symbol' – a methadone prescription is certification of being a 'junkie'
■ A source of income to buy heroin
■ Something to exchange for heroin
■ A way of keeping a partner with a more serious heroin problem stable
■ Help with their drug problem, believing that having a methadone prescription is the only way to get help.

Or they may be seeking a methadone prescription because they have been coerced by a:
■ Relative
■ Friend
■ Partner
■ Employer
■ Court.

Determining optimum treatment duration

The initial care plan should outline the anticipated duration of treatment. Clearly this can be modified over time but an agreement should be reached at the outset which outlines either the:
■ Planned treatment duration, or
■ Intervals at which it will be reviewed.

In 1990 the World Health Organisation convened a special meeting of international experts on methadone treatment and this group suggested a standard terminology for methadone treatment using these terms:
■ Short-term detoxification: decreasing doses over one month or less
■ Long-term detoxification: decreasing doses over more than one month
■ Short-term maintenance: stable prescribing over 6 months or less
■ Long-term maintenance: stable prescribing over more than 6 months.

The indications and contra-indications for these four categories are set out below.

Short-term detoxification

See also Section 9: Methadone detoxification.

Decreasing doses over one month or less

If methadone treatment is justified a minimum definition of successful short-term detox would be:

- Contact with helping services during the treatment period
- No illicit opiate/depressant drug use during the detoxification period
- No opiate use for 1 month following detox.

Factors that would indicate that short-term detox may be a successful treatment option	Factors that would indicate that short-term detox may not be a successful intervention
Strong motivation to become drug-free	Little motivation to become drug-free
Strong social support network	Poor social support network
Short history of opiate use	Long history of continuous opiate use
Low daily opiate use	High daily opiate use
High degree of control in opiate use	Low degree of control in opiate use
No other drugs being used	Poly drug use e.g. opiates. alcohol, benzodiazepines, etc.
Client requesting this treatment option of their own free will	Pressure from others to undergo treatment despite reluctance and anxiety
Client has a clear vision of what they are aiming for and of the benefits of being drug-free	Client only wants to be 'off opiates' and has not considered how to stay off
Availability of in-patient detox facility	Early or late pregnancy
Detox is part of a care plan which includes residential rehabilitation	Unavailability of in-patient detox facility
Client is smoking rather than injecting opiates	Compulsory detox following breach of prescribing contract

Long-term detoxification

See also Section 9: Methadone detoxification.

Decreasing doses over more than one month

If methadone treatment is justified, and short-term detox has been excluded, a minimum definition of successful long-term detox would be:

■ Contact with helping services during the treatment period

■ No illicit opiate/depressant drug use during the detoxification period

■ No opiate use for 1 month following detox.

Factors that would indicate that long-term detox may be a successful treatment option	Factors that would indicate that long-term detox may not be a successful intervention
Client determination to become drug-free with a recognition that other factors (physical, social, psychological) need working on as a pre-condition to successful outcome of the detox	Client requests to become drug-free without recognition of the factors which may cause relapse
Failure of short-term detox: particularly if withdrawal symptoms precipitate relapse	Long-standing chaotic, drug-using lifestyle
Client request for long-term detox	Little motivation to become drug-free
Desire to address psychological issues during the detox period	No desire to address psychological issues that may contribute to relapse
Social support system in place or that can be rebuilt by the end of the detox	No prospect of a social support network developing during the detox
Need and desire to stop injecting behaviour in addition to detoxing	Desire to use injected drugs in a controlled way following detox
Support available from a specialist and/or counselling drug service	No support available from a specialist drug and/or counselling service

Short-term maintenance

Stable prescribing over 6 months or less

If methadone treatment is justified, and short and long-term detox have been excluded as options, a minimum definition of successful short-term maintenance would be:
- Contact with helping services during the treatment period
- Maintenance of contact with services
- Cessation of high-risk injecting behaviour
- Reduction/cessation of other opiate and depressant drug use.

Factors that would indicate that short-term maintenance may be a successful treatment option	Factors that would indicate that short-term maintenance may not be a successful intervention
Continued opiate use following past short and/or long-term detoxes	Long-term, chaotic drug-using history
Client request for short-term maintenance	Long-term injecting drug use
Opiate use following or during detox	Previous failure of detox following short-term maintenance
Prospect of social, physical and psychological factors improving given a period of drug-using stability	Client cannot envisage an end to their drug use
Client desire to work at creating pre-conditions to successful detox	Client feels dependent on injecting
Client has no dependence on injecting	Intravenous drug use which has, in the past, proved difficult to stop
Support available from a specialist drug service	No support available from a specialist drug service

Long-term maintenance

Stable doses over more than 6 months

If methadone treatment is justified, and short and long-term detox and short-term maintenance have been excluded as options, a minimum definition of successful long-term maintenance would be:

■ Contact with helping services during the treatment period
■ Maintenance of contact with services
■ Cessation of high-risk injecting behaviour
■ Reduction/cessation of other opiate and depressant drug use.

Factors that would indicate that long-term maintenance may be an appropriate intervention

Long-term history of drug use (particularly if injecting)

Successful outcome of short-term maintenance but client still not ready to detox

Poor social support network

Client needs time to make considerable social or psychological changes in order to be able to successfully detox

Support available from a specialist drug service

Factors that would indicate that long-term maintenance may not be an appropriate intervention

Short-term history of opiate use

Client has no desire to stabilise drug taking and poly drug use is continuing

No previous history of methadone prescribing/detox

Client is apparently able and willing to reduce methadone consumption

No support available from a specialist drug service

Treatment setting

For more information on the services available see Section 1: The history of methadone prescribing – Services available in the UK today. This section looks at the areas to which each treatment setting is best and least suited in the context of making appropriate treatment choices.

Specialist centre prescribing

Specialist centres are usually most suited to managing:
- Large numbers of clients who could overwhelm smaller services
- Chaotic drug users who need high levels of supervision and support
- Difficult to manage clients who require treatment from specialised staff – such as clients with multiple drug use or concurrent mental health problems.

They are usually less suited to helping:
- People who work full time (if they are only open Monday–Friday, 9am–5pm)
- Rural areas with poor public transport
- Opiate users not part of the subculture
- People who are ambivalent about receiving help (they often have long waiting lists).

GPs prescribing alone

General practitioners working without the support of a consultant with a special interest in drugs or a community drug team are usually most suited to managing people who:
- They know
- Require short or medium-term detoxification
- Have no concurrent benzodiazepine or other drug dependence
- Are able to attend appointments and are otherwise stable.

They are less suited to prescribing for people who:
- Are temporary residents
- Are chaotic in their drug use and lifestyle
- Require maintenance prescribing
- Have a dependence on other drugs in addition to opiates.

GPs working with a community drug team

With specialist support from clinicians who can have regular contact with the client over and above their 5–10 minute weekly or fortnightly consultation, GPs can take on and treat a much wider range of clients who have drug problems. They are usually best suited for clients who:
- Are stable enough to deal with attending appointments on time
- Would find attending a specialist centre difficult
- Are on a stable methadone programme – either detoxing or maintenance.

They are usually less suited for people who:
- Are chaotic and find attending appointments difficult
- Require supervised consumption of their methadone.

Private practice

Standards in private practice probably vary more than in other types of service for opiate users. Although all the questions below are legitimate questions to ask of any service if you are referring to, or receiving a client from, a private practice the following questions will help you ascertain the type and quality of the service on offer:
- Is it a group or single-handed practice?
- Have the staff recieved training in drug dependence?
- Are there written prescribing policies?
- What are the methadone collection regimes?
- What is the degree of contact and supervision of clients?
- Are counsellors and psychological support available and part of the treatment?
- Is there any liaison with the local statutory service and contact with the drug unit consultants?
- Are there limits on dosage and formulation?
- How is dosage calculated?
- What is the referral procedure?
- Is there a waiting list?
- What is the assessment procedure?
- What is the average case load per clinician?

- Are Home Office guidelines followed, such as requesting proof of a client's ability to fund their consultation and pharmacy fees?
- What is the catchment area of the practice?
- What are the fees and do they include, urinalysis as well as the consultation, and counselling?
- Are general practitioners kept informed?
- What information is given on treatment issues such as HIV and AIDS?

In general, responsible, well-supported and informed private practitioners are best suited for prescribing to people who:
- Are in full-time, well-paid employment
- Have legitimate access to funds to pay for treatment
- Are stable
- Will benefit from treatment not normally available on the NHS, such as injectables.

They are less suited to prescribing for people who:
- Have no legitimate access to funds
- Are chaotic and seeking maximum possible prescribed medication for least contact with helping services.

Prescribing injectable methadone

There are strong arguments for and against the principle of prescribing injectable methadone which are set out below.

Arguments used for prescribing injectable methadone	Arguments used against prescribing injectable methadone
It is an incentive for people who may not attend a service offering only oral methadone	It is difficult to determine who will benefit from prescribed injectables as there is no clear research or guidelines
It is an opportunity to work on a harm reduction basis with people who might not otherwise be in treatment	People may have stabilised well (and with less harm) on oral medication
It is a realistic prescribing response to people who cannot stop injecting	If decisions are made on prescribers' preferences – in the absence of guidelines – it will be a constant source of conflict
It may attract users into treatment earlier in their career	Clinicians can feel more like legal dealers and could attract more people than they could cope with into services
Giving clients a menu of drug choices can be empowering	Giving clients more choice can reduce the therapeutic value of services and leave clinicians feeling de-skilled
It can provide a way of stopping using intravenous heroin	It can cultivate or perpetuate injecting behaviour
It is a useful addition to an oral methadone prescription if occasional injecting behaviour persists	It can be seen as doctors approving of, and colluding with, dangerous behaviour
It could be cost effective if it prevents people from catching HIV	It may be seen by politicians and the media as 'being soft' on drugs and provide the springboard for a backlash that could threaten all prescribing
	Injectables on the illicit market would be even more dangerous than methadone mixture

If, having considered the pros and cons of prescribing injectables, a service has decided to offer injectable methadone as a treatment option, the indications and contra-indications are set out below.

Factors that would indicate that prescribing injectable methadone may be an appropriate intervention	**Factors that would indicate that prescribing injectable methadone may not be an appropriate intervention**
Client continuing to inject illicit opiate drugs despite 6 months or more on over 80mg oral methadone daily	Client has no experience of oral methadone treatment
Long history of injecting	Short history of injecting
Client only injecting opiates in addition to their methadone	Client injecting many drugs in addition to taking their oral methadone
Client has long-term contact with the drug service	Client is a new referral or temporary resident

Diamorphine prescribing

As with the prescription of injectables there are strong arguments for and against the principle of prescribing the user's drug of choice which are set out below.

Arguments used for prescribing diamorphine (heroin)

Heroin, especially if smoked, is less likely to cause accidental overdose than methadone

It would attract many of the people who are most at risk of HIV and other drug-related harm into contact with drug services

This is a catch 22 situation: while 'the establishment' opposes heroin prescribing, research funding is not available to prove the improved efficacy its proponents expect

It is for clinicians to inform policy makers of the most effective forms of health care: reduced crime and HIV spread are easy positive outcomes to 'sell' to opponents of prescribing

Arguments used against prescribing diamorphine (heroin)

As opiate users who are more chaotic are attracted into services there is more likelihood that the prescribed drugs will just increase the total drug consumption

The number of people who would request treatment with heroin could overwhelm services

There is little research to demonstrate that it would be an effective intervention

As with prescribing injectables, prescribing heroin could provide the basis for a reactionary backlash against all prescribing and services for drug users

The prescribing of diamorphine in the treatment of dependence is restricted to those doctors who have a Home Office licence to do so. If, having considered the pros and cons of prescribing diamorphine, a service has decided to offer it as a treatment option, the indications and contra-indications are set out below.

Factors that may indicate that prescribing diamorphine would be an appropriate intervention

Heroin has been the drug of choice over a long period of time

Client has a long history of injecting

Client has continued to inject heroin regularly in addition to taking oral methadone

Client has continued injecting despite receiving 80mg or more of methadone for more than 6 months

Client has long-term contact with the service

Additional risk from injecting practice due to HIV-positive status

Client is already on a diamorphine prescription

Factors that may indicate that prescribing diamorphine may not be an appropriate intervention

Client also injects drugs other than heroin on a regular basis

Client has a short history of injecting

Client occasionally injects opiates in addition to taking oral methadone

Client has continued injecting on a low dose of oral methadone

Client is new to the service or a temporary resident

Client is reluctant to engage with the service and a diamorphine prescription is unlikely to improve this

103

summary

- Treatment should aim to reduce drug-related harm.

- The client's motivation to change the component behaviours of their drug taking, as well as their desire to achieve abstinence, must inform the treatment choices made.

- Appropriate treatment duration is a key factor in achieving positive outcomes.

- The indications for treatment should be carefully considered following a thorough assessment.

- Methadone should only be used in the treatment of people who are opiate dependent.

- Prescribing medication other than oral methadone mixture for the treatment of opiate dependence is controversial and should normally be undertaken only by a specialist service.

The decision about what treatment to offer is based on:
- What is available
- The client's previous history
- The client's current circumstances

and the clinician's judgement of the required degree of:
- Structure
- Monitoring
- Support.

section 8

Getting the

starting

dose right

Factors in determining the starting dose **106**

The dangers of prescribing too much/not enough **107**

How much methadone should you prescribe? **108**

Methadone equivalent doses **109**

Dose titration **112**

Summary **113**

Introduction

Having decided to commence methadone treatment, calculation of the correct starting dose when commencing treatment is a difficult and contentious issue. This section is mainly intended to give guidance to the non-specialist prescriber as to the principles governing calculation of the appropriate methadone dose.

Before methadone treatment can commence there must be a full and thorough assessment and clear treatment aims must be defined.

The decision as to how much methadone a person should be prescribed is not simply a calculation of the equivalent dose of methadone to the amount of opiates they are taking.

For these reasons this section must not be read in isolation but in the context of the rest of the book, particularly:
- Section 2: The research basis for methadone prescribing
- Section 6: Assessment
- Section 7: Treatment aims and choices.

Factors in determining the starting dose

The calculation of the 'right dose' must take into account the following factors:
- The 'right dose' varies according to the treatment aim
- Illicit heroin varies in purity from area to area and from time to time
- Clients may exaggerate their drug usage to obtain more methadone
- Workers may underestimate clients' drug use to reduce the amount of methadone they prescribe
- Methadone is a long-acting opiate
- Too much methadone can be fatal or lead to illicit sale but insufficient methadone is unlikely to be effective.

These factors are dealt with in more detail below.

Treatment aims

The optimum amount of methadone for each person will vary within a given range according to the amount of opiates they are taking and the agreed treatment aims. If the chosen treatment option is detox then the aim will be to determine the minimum daily dose of methadone that will keep the client free of withdrawal symptoms.

If the client is an intravenous user and the treatment aim is to use methadone to help them stop injecting, by giving them enough to greatly reduce the desire to use heroin, then they will probably need more methadone than someone who was smoking the same quantity of heroin per day.

Variations in heroin purity

Variations in heroin from area to area tend, on the whole, to remain fairly constant – purity levels in London would typically be consistently higher than purity levels in the provinces.

Batch to batch purity can change – generally with a given area experiencing a week or so of supplies of 'bad' heroin i.e. below average purity, every now and then, or, conversely, a week or two of 'good' heroin i.e. above average purity.

However, on the whole, agencies who do a lot of prescribing within a given locality retain a fairly constant baseline conversion level of heroin to methadone for people who want to detox.

Exaggeration of drug usage by clients

As the accurate determination of actual drug usage and tolerance are essential components of any prescribing assessment this issue is discussed in detail in Section 6: Assessment.

Deliberate underestimation of drug use

Many drug services have ceilings (both official and unofficial) as to the amount of methadone they will prescribe. In such cases it can be tempting to disbelieve a client's estimation of their drug use in order to justify prescribing a sub therapeutic dose. However it is better for both client and worker for prescribing ceilings (where they exist) to be made explicit in the assessment process, and to directly address any difficulties this may cause.

Methadone is a long-acting drug

Methadone's long action can cause problems: (see Section 4: Physiology and pharmacology of methadone)
■ Methadone feels different to heroin
■ The slow onset of action is markedly different from heroin
■ Methadone builds up in the system over the first 3 days.

Methadone feels different to heroin

Clients often expect (or hope) that, as a heroin substitute, methadone will make them feel similar. Lack of understanding of this phenomenon is often a feature of high-dose requests from clients who come for their first methadone prescription. In the past they may have taken large quantities of illicit methadone on a one-off basis and found that they did not experience the usual opiate euphoria. They often conclude from this experience that they need much more than they had before in order to replace the heroin they are using. When it doesn't, they often believe a higher dose will achieve the same feelings.

In fact for most people the experiences are qualitatively different with no initial 'rush' following consumption and a reduced euphoric effect. A larger dose of methadone only makes people feel like they have had more methadone – it does not make them feel like they have taken heroin.

Methadone has a slow onset of action

The physiology of this phenomenon is described in Section 4. This causes two problems. Firstly people who have taken illicit methadone on an occasional basis may believe that they need a larger dose than they really do in order to achieve absence of withdrawal symptoms. Secondly, clients get maximum effect from the methadone about 72 hours into treatment when they usually want maximum effect within a few hours.

These problems can be largely resolved, and clients helped to accept a realistic therapeutic dose, by giving an understanding of the issues, and by clinicians acknowledging the psychological pressures which exist for clients who are making the transition from heroin to methadone.

The dangers of prescribing too much/not enough

Accidental overdose

Accidental overdose is one of the greatest risks of methadone prescribing.

Patients who cannot be observed for at least 4 hours following administration of the first dose of methadone should not be allowed to take a dose greater than the minimum lethal dose of 50mg. If there is any risk of the use of alcohol or other depressants prescribers must bear in mind that the lethal dose will be lower still.

Illicit sales

A certain amount of illicit selling of methadone is an unavoidable consequence of any methadone prescribing programme that allows clients unsupervised methadone consumption. It is commonly referred to as 'spillage' or 'leakage'.

Sale of the initial doses will occur only if the initial assessment has seriously over estimated the amount of methadone required and/or the client's intentions to switch to methadone treatment.

At the start of methadone treatment leakage to the illicit market is less likely and can be minimised by careful prescribing and monitoring of the client in the early stages of their treatment.

Not prescribing enough

Opiate users presenting for methadone treatment will have a clear expectation that methadone will 'hold' them and prevent them experiencing withdrawals. Education about what to expect over the first few days of treatment (see above) cannot compensate for an inadequate dose, the result of which is likely to be continued illicit drug use and/or dropping out of treatment.

How much methadone should you prescribe?

If you have decided to prescribe methadone and have reached a conclusion about:
■ The amount of opiates you believe the client to be using
■ The treatment aims

you then need to make a calculation as to the appropriate therapeutic dose.

If the client is using prescribed pharmaceutical opiates then the conversion is fairly easy. However this is rarely the case. With illicit drug users assessment of actual drug use is discussed at length in the suceeding section.

For non-specialist prescribers the essential rules to remember are:
■ Start on a safe, low dose and work up
■ The lethal dose for a non-tolerant adult is around 50mg
■ If in doubt refer to a specialist drug service and/or prolong the assessment period.

Non-specialist prescribers should not prescribe collected doses of more than 50mg until tolerance has been established.

Where the starting dose is pitched the range of equivalent doses will depend on factors such as:
■ The amount of control the person has over their drug use
■ The level of motivation to stop using illicit opiates
■ Whether or not they inject
■ How soon it is planned to reduce the methadone dose
■ The risk of overdose
■ Anticipated concurrent alcohol/other depressant drug consumption.

It is always important to bear in mind that it is easier to increase the dose after the first week of treatment if it is proving insufficient than to reduce it if you think it is too much and the client disagrees!

Methadone equivalent doses

It is not possible to directly convert the effects, duration and dependence potential of other opiates to a fixed equivalent in methadone. Therefore these charts must be used with caution and in conjunction with the explanatory text above.

Pharmaceutical opiates

Equivalent oral dose[50]	Preparation	Route	Methadone dose
Diamorphine (heroin)	IV	10mg ampoule	20mg
		30mg ampoule	50mg
	Oral	10mg	20mg
Methadone	IV	10mg ampoule	10mg
Morphine	IV	10mg ampoule	10mg
	Oral	10mg	10mg
	Rectal	10mg	10mg
Dipipanone (Diconal)	Oral	10mg	4mg
Dihydrocodeine (DF118)	Oral	30mg	3mg
Dextromoramide (Palfium)	Oral	5mg	5–10mg
		10mg	10–20mg
Pethidine	IV	50mg ampoule	5mg
	Oral	50mg	5mg
Buprenorphine (Temgesic)	IV	300 microgram ampoule	8mg
	Oral	200 microgram tablet	5mg
Pentazocine (Fortral)	Oral	25mg tablet	2mg
		50mg capsule	4mg
Codeine linctus 100mL	Oral	300mg codeine phosphate	10mg
Codeine phosphate	Oral	15mg tablet	1mg
		30mg tablet	2mg
		60mg tablet	3mg
Gee's linctus 100mL	Oral	16mg anhydrous morphine	10mg
J Collis Brown 100mL	Oral	10mg extract of opium	10mg

Illicit heroin to methadone conversion

Conversion of illicit heroin consumption into an appropriate methadone dose is complicated by all the factors outlined above and in Section 6: Assessment. It varies widely according to local practice.

This table is a guide only and should not be used without consultation with your local drugs service.

There is room on the table for you to add the optimum dose for your service. It is filled in here with approximate values which give a typical range for the figures.

Illicit heroin conversion chart

Daily spend on heroin	Amount used in grams	Route	Starting methadone dose – detox	Starting methadone dose – stabilise
£10	1/8th	Smoked	0–10mg	5–25mg
		IV	0–25mg	5–25mg
£20	0.25g	Smoked	10–25mg	10–40mg
		IV	15–35mg	15–45mg
£40	0.5g	Smoked	15–50mg	20–50mg
		IV	25–60mg	30–65mg
£50	0.75g	Smoked	25–65mg	30–70mg
		IV	25–70mg	35–75mg
£80	1.0g	Smoked	30–80mg	35–85mg
		IV	30–90mg	35–100mg
£100	1.5g	Smoked	45–100mg	45–120mg
		IV	45–110mg	45–130mg
£150	2.0g	Smoked	50–120mg	50–130mg
		IV	50–120mg	50–130mg

Ounces to grams conversion

Heroin is bulk bought in fractions of an ounce, if a client is referring to their consumption in ounces use the conversion chart below to convert back to grams.

Ounces to grams conversion chart

Ounces	Grams equivalent
Half (0.5)	14g
Quarter (0.25)	7g
Eighth (0.12)	3.5g
Sixteenth (0.063)	1.75g

Dose titration

The aim is to titrate the methadone dose against any signs of withdrawal and cravings for or actual illicit opiate use, during the first three days of treatment. The client should be seen regularly to assess whether any withdrawal signs are present. If these are observed the daily dosage can be increased by up to 10-20%. By the third day the total daily dose should provide a reasonable baseline for either a reduction or longer-term prescribing.

Administration of the initial dose

This can be given either as a single dose or divided into 2 doses 12 hours apart. Either way it is preferable to observe the client for at least 2 hours after the first dose to ensure they do not become intoxicated and so reduce the risk of overdose. If there are signs of intoxication the observation period should be extended to 4 hours and consideration should be given to reducing the dose.

As it is not always possible to estimate accurately the equivalent dose of street heroin some practitioners (usually those with access to in-patient facilities) start with a dose of 20mg methadone and observe. If withdrawal signs remain 2–4 hours after this dose a further 20 mg is given and so on, up to a usual maximum of 50 mg in the first 24 hours. The first day's total dose is the starting point for day 2 and any further increases are titrated against withdrawal signs.

Opiate users – particularly those who have been using high doses of illicit methadone – may have a very high tolerance and be able to take doses in excess of 100mg without appearing intoxicated. Dose titration should therefore be against cessation of withdrawal symptoms rather than indications of intoxication.

Also remember that people who have had a break from regular opiate use, perhaps through detox or a prison sentence, and are asking for methadone in the early stages of relapse to illicit heroin use may have a much lower tolerance for methadone than they think.

summary

■ Methadone is a potentially lethal drug.

■ Prescribers should avoid allowing patients to take away initial doses of methadone sufficient to cause accidental overdose i.e. 50mg or less, if there is concurrent benzodiazepine or alcohol use.

■ If you are in the position of having to make a decision about prescribing and you have any doubt in your mind, it is better to be safe than sorry. Refer to a specialist drugs service or doctor with experience for a second opinion.

■ Ask your local drugs agency to help you fill in the equivalent dose ranges for the illicit heroin to methadone chart.

■ Always titrate the dose against prevention of withdrawal symptoms and reduction in cravings for illicit opiates rather than against the observable intoxication.

■ Start off with the lowest workable dose based on a thorough assessment and increase if necessary.

section 9

Methadone

detoxification

Reasons for detoxing **116**

Blind or open reductions? **118**

Setting the appropriate rate of detox **119**

Detox regime suggestions **120**

Anxiety **122**

Abstinence phobia **122**

Alternatives to methadone
in detoxification **122**

Methadone v heroin in detoxification **125**

Follow up/relapse prevention **126**

Summary **127**

Introduction

Methadone detoxification is a complex area dealt with in various sections throughout this book.

This section deals with the practical issues around prescribing and the rate of detox, the anxieties for clients about detox and the alternatives to methadone in detox.

This section should be read in conjunction with:
- Section 2 – where there is a discussion of the research into methadone detoxification
- Section 4 – where withdrawal symptoms are discussed
- Section 7 – where there is discussion of the different detox durations and their indications and contra-indications
- Section 11 – where there is discussion of detoxification which does not end in lasting abstinence.

People reducing from methadone are often anxious and afraid of the withdrawal syndrome and relapse.

Relapse following detox is an often neglected area because drug services and drug users tend to concentrate on the withdrawal syndrome and process of detoxification.

Effective follow up is vital in ensuring that detoxification is more than a reducing dose of methadone mirrored by a concurrent rise in heroin (or other depressant drug) use or a prelude to a short period of abstinence followed by relapse that the prescriber is unaware of.

Information for clients on the issues around detoxification and residential rehabilitation is available in the *Detox Handbook* and the *Rehab Handbook* – also available from ISDD (address on back cover).

Reasons for detoxing

In an ideal world people would detox from a stabilising dose of methadone or illicit drugs when they, and their prescriber, agreed that they were ready and able to do so without significant risk of early relapse. However people may want to detox when either they or their prescriber do not feel they are ready because:
- Service prescribing policy dictates the regime on offer
- They have a new job
- They are moving to a new area
- Of changes in their relationship
- Attitudes of staff involved in methadone prescribing
- Unrealistic staff beliefs about client's ability to achieve abstinence
- Unrealistic client beliefs about their ability to achieve abstinence
- Stigma associated with having a methadone prescription
- Dislike of practical aspects of a regime, such as the collection frequency
- Change of drug of choice e.g. methadone to benzodiazepines or alcohol
- Exclusion from a prescribing programme
- Imminent or actual prison sentence.

These are discussed below.

Attitudes of staff
Opiate users are sensitive to the attitudes of the staff they come into contact with and sometimes choose not to seek, or to terminate treatment because of the attitudes and behaviour of staff.

This can probably be best avoided by offering services that are:
- Client centred
- Empowering
- Flexible in their treatment approaches
- Not seen to subscribe rigidly to any duration of methadone treatment
- Non-judgmental and respectful
- Staffed by people who are well trained and receive good supervision.

Following these principles also means that, having discussed the options, if a client decides to detoxify against advice the staff should still offer their full support and encouragement during and after the detox. They should also endeavour to discuss possible outcomes in a way that does not set the client up to fail but allows the making of contingency plans that can be brought into play if the detox does not work.

Unrealistic staff beliefs about a client's ability to detox

It is easy for workers to fall into the trap of prematurely believing that people can achieve abstinence and encourage the client to detox. Often the client will continue down this road because they do not want to upset the worker and this can continue afterwards, with the client not wishing to re-refer themselves to a prescribing service for fear of admonishment from, or upsetting, the people who helped them before.

Cushman and Dole[87] found that of a group of methadone maintenance clients who were assessed as 'rehabilitated' and detoxed with the anticipation of success, some asked to be returned to maintenance during the detox and 25% returned to maintenance after detox (mainly because of protracted withdrawals).

Therefore support, encouragement and optimism should always be tempered by continual reassessment and meaningful negotiation.

Unrealistic client beliefs about their ability to detox

Clients too can be unrealistically optimistic about their ability to get off opiates. Often people will present after many years of heavy opiate use, adamant that in a few weeks they will be able to get themselves together and detox successfully.[88]

This belief sometimes stems from concentrating on the physical aspects of opiate withdrawal. If past experience of relapse during or after opiate detox has been that the withdrawal symptoms were the main

factor causing relapse, this can reinforce the belief that if the physical symptoms of withdrawal can be reduced to tolerable levels by a methadone detox, abstinence will be easily achieved.

Another factor can be the flawed but understandable and apparently logical conclusion that 'if all my problems are heroin-related then if I give up heroin all my problems will go away'. The experience of many is that the compulsive behavioural aspects of their drug taking and the social and emotional difficulties that they experience once opiate-free add a previously ignored and difficult-to-overcome dimension to their drug use.

Stigma associated with having a methadone prescription

Many people on a maintenance methadone prescribing programme say 'the act of having to take an opiate every day is a reminder that I'm a junkie'.

For the relatives and friends of people on methadone it can be perceived as being 'as bad as heroin' – regardless of any associated lifestyle improvements that have been achieved. Indeed associated improvements often serve only to increase the pressure on the person to detox as the perception is that they do not need the methadone anymore.

Heroin users are often dismissive of those on methadone and street myths of the terrible long-term health consequences of methadone treatment still abound. So the person receiving methadone often feels stigmatised from all sides.

Heroin users who feel the need to seek help for the first time also feel this and may request a methadone detox so that they can rationalise their request as one for a short-lived intervention that does not involve long-term methadone treatment.

Dislike of practical aspects of a regime, such as the collection frequency

Avoidance of longer-term treatment may also include factors such as a desire not to have to:

■ Collect methadone daily from a drug service or pharmacy.
■ Attend a drug service on a regular basis
■ Engage in a counselling relationship
■ See other drug users when collecting the prescription and/or methadone

It is important for the worker involved to have an awareness of these issues if they are factors in a request for methadone detoxification.

Change of drug of choice

Sometimes poly drug users change their drug of choice in a cyclical way from, say, heroin to benzodiazepines to alcohol to amphetamines and back to heroin; or simply switch from heroin to, say, alcohol and back again.

They may ask for a detox at the end of the opiate part of the cycle – either as a new referral as a heroin user or following a period on methadone. In these cases treatment may or may not be appropriate, but if commenced should be carefully monitored.

Clients going to prison

Clients who have a prison sentence coming up present drug services with a dilemma. On the one hand premature detox may lead to relapse with risk behaviour prior to prison. On the other hand arriving at a prison where detox facilities are poor or non-existent in full methadone withdrawal is likely to result in illicit heroin use. The sharing of injecting equipment in prison is much more prevalent than in the community.
The best that can be done is to:
■ Offer as much support as possible
■ Help them make informed choices
■ Inform them of the risks of intravenous drug use in prison
■ Appropriately influence the pre-sentence report.

Blind or open reductions?

There is no evidence to suggest that knowing or not knowing the frequency or size of dose reductions is more effective in helping people detox using methadone.

The answer for most people who attend prescribing and dispensing services that are flexible enough to offer both, is to consider the pros and cons of each approach in conjunction with the prescribing staff, and to make an informed decision for themselves as to which is the most appropriate regime. Generally a key factor is the level of control that a person feels they have over their lives. Anyone who feels in control is unlikely to opt for blind dose reductions.

The arguments for and against blind and open reductions are set out below.

Arguments for blind dose reductions

Reduced anxiety around the day of dose reduction

Objective self assessment of withdrawal symptoms

Concentration on issues around coping rather than drug dose

Reduced anxiety about passing psychologically important doses e.g. 20mg,10mg, 5mg

Arguments against blind dose reductions

Possible constant anxiety about when reductions are going to happen

Constant anxiety about and experience of withdrawal symptoms

Client not taking responsibility for the dose reductions or their response to them

Inability to 'take credit' for success so far

Arguments for open dose reductions

Client takes responsibility for the dose reductions and their response to them

Ability to plan life around reductions

The rate of reduction can be negotiated once detox has started

Arguments against open dose reductions

Increased anxiety and expectations of withdrawal symptoms at times of dose reductions

Weeks of concentration on drug dose as the major factor in determining ability to function is not always helpful preparation for a drug-free life

Client is more able to identify psychologically significant doses at which to stop – which can weaken resolve

Setting the appropriate rate of detox

Almost everyone undergoing methadone detoxification will experience withdrawal symptoms, and for many these will be serious enough to be a major contributing factor in either relapse to heroin use or a request for methadone maintenance – even if all other preconditions for a successful detox are in place.[87]

For people detoxing following a period on methadone maintenance, faster detoxes are associated with higher drop-out rates and slower detoxes are associated with lower drop-out rates.[89]

In general detoxes consist of gradual reductions of 5mg or 10mg in the daily dose to a given level, usually 20–30mg (depending on the starting dose and the client), and then become more gradual, either in terms of time between reductions and/or size of daily dose reduction.

Negotiation between worker and client is an important component of any detoxification. A negotiated detoxification in which the client is able to take responsibility for coping with the dose reductions is likely to reduce the risk of concurrent illicit opiate use and be a better foundation for continued abstinence afterwards.

Prescribers without specialist experience who agree to a short-term programme without support from a specialist service should seek support if their patient is unable to detox successfully at the agreed rate.

Detox regime suggestions

All the regimes below are for methadone mixture 1mg/1mL. All detox regimes are a plan only and should be subject to regular, i.e. weekly or fortnightly, review against the treatment aims.

The definitions, indications and contra-indications for each of the regimes below are given in Section 7 – Treatment aims and choices. It is important that detox regimes are only entered into with clear treatment aims and following a thorough assessment that has established that these aims are achievable.

The very low doses (i.e. less than 5mg) suggested in the following regimes are of little physiological value as they are unlikely to make much difference to the level of physical withdrawal. However withdrawal symptoms can also be aggravated by anxiety and where low dose prescribing at the end of a detox reduces anxiety it is likely to reduce subjectively experienced withdrawals.

Where a client has high levels of anxiety about making the final reductions they are often afraid of being drug free and of the changes this will bring. It is therefore important that low dose prescribing is coupled with counselling.

Short-term detoxification: decreasing doses over one month or less
Two week detoxification regime
- 20mg for 3 days
- 15mg for 4 days
- 10mg for 3 days
- 5mg for 4 days

This regime has the advantage that it is easy to prescribe as there is a dose drop at the end of each week.

An alternative starting slightly higher could be:
- 25mg for 3 days
- 20mg for 3 days
- 15mg for 3 days
- 10mg for 3 days
- 5mg for 2 days

For people who need more methadone to stabilise or who are detoxing from an existing methadone prescription there are two main choices. Either reduce the dose prior to the final detox or reduce the dose by 25%–50% each day until 20mg is reached and then complete the programme as above. However it must be recognised that these large early reductions will probably result in intense withdrawal symptoms.

If required, 'holding' on a given dose on one or two occasions during the detox may increase the client's sense of control and decrease their anxiety. Delays in the rate of reduction should usually be accompanied by an increase in psychological support.

Longer-term detoxification: decreasing doses over 1–6 months
1 month detoxification regime
From a starting dose of 40mg:
- 40mg for 4 days
- 35mg for 3 days
- 30mg for 4 days
- 25mg for 3 days
- 20mg for 4 days
- 15mg for 3 days
- 10mg for 4 days
- 5mg for 3 days

From a starting dose of 25mg:
- 25 mg for 4 days
- 20mg for 3 days
- 15mg for 4 days
- 10mg for 3 days
- 8mg for 4 days
- 6mg for 3 days
- 4mg for 4 days
- 2mg for 3 days

4 month detoxification regime

Following initial stabilisation, and a period in which the client remains heroin free, the daily dose can be reduced by 5mg or 10mg every week or fortnight until 30mg is reached.

The rate of reduction in the daily dose is then reduced to 5mg every week or fortnight until 10–15mg is reached. At this point daily dose reductions can be reduced to 2 or 2.5mg every week or fortnight.

A typical 4 month regime using these principles from a starting dose of 45mg would be:

- 45mg for 14 days
- 35mg for 14 days

- 30mg for 14 days
- 25mg for 14 days

- 20mg for 14 days
- 15mg for 14 days

- 10mg for 14 days
- 7mg for 14 days

6 month detoxification regime

A 6 month detox regime using the same principles as the 1–5 month detox, from a start of 60mg might be:

- 60mg for 14 days
- 50mg for 14 days

- 40mg for 14 days
- 30mg for 14 days

- 25mg for 14 days
- 20mg for 14 days

- 15mg for 14 days
- 10mg for 14 days

- 8mg for 14 days
- 6mg for 14 days

- 4mg for 14 days
- 2mg for 14 days

Detoxification following exclusion from a methadone prescribing programme

Sometimes methadone prescriptions are stopped. The reasons for doing this are discussed in Section 10: Practical issues in methadone prescribing – Terminating treatment.

The client should be aware of exactly what the rate of detox will be before the prescription is terminated. Abrupt cessation of opiates is not fatal in people who are otherwise healthy. The rate of reduction therefore usually seeks to strike a balance between continuance of the prescribing programme under a new guise, and a rate of reduction which gives the individual little chance of achieving abstinence if they want to.

A regime such as the following is commonly used:

- 10mg reduction in the daily dose every day until the patient is receiving 30mgs daily

and then:

- 5mg reduction in the daily dose each day with 2 days on 5mg at the end.

However any of the above regimes could be employed.

Anxiety

Client expectations of anxiety are one of the best indicators of the intensity of withdrawal symptoms and there can be little doubt that the two are closely linked.

As with all anxiety-provoking situations, levels of anxiety during and after methadone detoxification can be reduced through information being given to the client about what they can expect to happen and why it is happening, and the opportunity being given to discuss the issues that are raised.

Emotions such as anger and depression can trigger withdrawal symptoms in people who are stabilised on methadone – this is known as 'pseudo withdrawal syndrome'. If clients become more aware of these feelings during a detox then this too will increase the severity of their withdrawal symptoms. Counselling during and after the detox can help deal with these emotions and reduce the physical consequences.

Abstinence phobia

S M Hall in 1979 described abstinence phobia as an exaggerated response to comparatively mild withdrawal symptoms.[90]

Indeed many clients become very anxious as soon as dose reductions begin and feel unable to continue with the detoxification. Hall suggested that previous actual or observed traumatic experience of withdrawal symptoms may be the cause of this fear. Unfortunately her attempts to use standard cognitive behavioural therapy in a controlled trial – which has been shown to be effective in other anxiety disorders – were unsuccessful.

This being the case, choices for clients who demonstrate high levels of anxiety during detox are limited as they are unlikely to achieve abstinence without considerable support. Slowing the rate of reduction and increasing support is the first line response. Following this in-patient detoxification or residential rehabilitation might be options.

If the anxiety cannot be resolved, and relapse is the outcome of all attempts at detox, the most appropriate response may be methadone maintenance.

Alternatives to methadone in detoxification

Clonidine

This is similar in its action to lofexidine (see below), the major difference being its more powerful hypotensive action which contra-indicates its use in anything other than an in-patient setting. Clonidine has never had a product licence for opiate detoxification.

Lofexidine (BritLofex)

Lofexidine hydrochloride is now fully licensed in the UK for management of the symptoms caused by withdrawal. Lofexidine is not an opiate and does not stimulate opiate receptors and therefore does not have the psychoactive effect nor the dependency potential of opiates.

It works by inhibiting the release of noradrenaline. Noradrenaline is a key chemical transmitter that acts on the nervous system, the action of which has been suppressed by opiates: see Section 4: The physiology and pharmacology of methadone.

As lofexidine is not an opiate, increasing the dose too quickly, or beyond the recommended maximum, will not necessarily reduce withdrawal symptoms but it will increase the risk of side effects such as hypotension (low blood pressure). This should be made very clear to patients who are self administering their lofexidine tablets.

The safety of lofexidine in pregnancy has not yet been established.

Lofexidine is unlikely to:
- Completely eliminate withdrawal symptoms (the extent to which it reduces withdrawal symptoms varies)
- Greatly affect the insomnia associated with opiate withdrawal
- Stop cravings for opiates
- Reduce anxiety
- Be effective if used in the absence of careful assessment and support during and after treatment.

The effect of these factors can be reduced by:
- Giving the client full information about what to expect
- Using low-dose prescribed night sedation for a defined period (lofexidine may potentiate the action of anxiolytics and hypnotics)
- Offering support and counselling during and after the detox.

Side effects

Hypotension (low blood pressure) is the principle possible side effect that can occur during treatment with lofexidine. Although this could prohibit its use for some clients and may result in discontinuation of treatment in others, in practice there is rarely a clinically significant reduction in blood pressure.

Blood pressure should be monitored, especially while the dose is increasing. For in-patients if the standing systolic BP has dropped by more than 30 mmHg (and is associated with symptoms of dizziness and light-headedness or over-sedation) the next dose of lofexidine should be withheld until the systolic BP is less than 30mmHg below the baseline.

Sedation is more likely to occur in clients concurrently prescribed (or taking) benzodiazepines and/or other central nervous system depressants.

Lofexidine is safe for community use in patients who are:
- Able to control their use of the drug
- Unlikely to use illicit drugs concurrently
- Willing to comply with the regime
- In regular contact with the prescriber/drug worker.

A typical 10 day out-patient lofexidine regime

Reduce the methadone dose to 15mg daily and ask the patient to take their last dose in the evening.

The following morning (detox day 1) begin the following regime:
(see over)

123

Day of detox	Maximum number of tablets to be taken in the morning	Maximum number of tablets to be taken at lunch time	Maximum number of tablets to be taken at 6pm	Maximum number of tablets to be taken at night
Day 1	2	0	0	2
Day 2	2	0	2	2
Day 3	2	2	2	2
Day 4	3	2	2	3
Day 5	3	3	3	3
Day 6	3	1	2	3
Day 7	2	0	2	3
Day 8	2	0	1	2
Day 9	1	0	0	1
Day 10	0	0	0	1

Notes:

■ The action of lofexidine is reduced by tricyclic antidepressants and they should not, therefore, be prescribed concurrently.

■ Patients may determine their own dose, titrated against withdrawal symptoms, up to the maximum doses shown.

■ Blood pressure and pulse should be monitored regularly, especially while the dose is increasing.

■ The maximum dose phase i.e. 'Day 5' may be continued for up to 6 days prior to beginning the 'Day 6–10' reduction regime if withdrawals remain severe or if there has been additional illicit drug use.

The patient must be told:

■ To omit or take less than the maximum dose if giddiness is a problem

■ That once the maximum dose is reached taking more tablets will only increase the side effects and will not further diminish the withdrawal symptoms

■ That the worst withdrawal symptoms will be experienced on days 1–5

■ That there may be an immediate drop in tolerance to opiates – so if they relapse, the risk of overdose will be high.

Dihydrocodeine
In an attempt to reduce the severity of withdrawal symptoms some services switch detoxifying clients from methadone to dihydrocodeine for the final part of the process – usually when the daily methadone dose reaches around 15mg.

The rationale for this is that dihydrocodeine is:
- A shorter-acting drug that may interfere with natural endorphin production less than methadone, thus reducing the severity of long-term withdrawals
- A relatively weak opiate (30mg of dihydrocodeine = 3mg of methadone)
- Easy to reduce slowly without practical difficulties, especially if the 10mg/5mL elixir is used.

There have been no controlled trials comparing subjective experience of withdrawals when detoxing on methadone, heroin or dihydrocodeine, but some clinicians have found the switch helpful, particularly if the anxiety of withdrawal is focused on the problems of coming off methadone.

However the treatment can have drawbacks. The experience of a 'high' on dihydrocodeine can be greater than with methadone and thus clients can attempt unsustainable methadone dose reductions in pursuit of the 'reward' of a 'better drug'.

Switching drug can also detract from the other psychological causes of withdrawal symptoms, neglect of which is unlikely to be therapeutic.

The product licence for dihydrocodeine does not include treatment of opiate dependence.

Methadone v heroin in detoxification

There is a commonly held belief amongst drug users that the withdrawal symptoms are worse and more prolonged when coming off methadone than heroin.

Given that methadone is a longer-acting drug this is probably true. However the experience of withdrawal is probably exacerbated by factors which are different with regard to most methadone detoxes as opposed to most illicit heroin detoxes.

Most illicit heroin withdrawal symptoms are:
- Part of a fluctuating drug-using pattern and associated with shortages of heroin
- Result in only a few days' abstinence
- Self-medicated, to some extent, with benzodiazepines, alcohol or other drugs
- Not part of a planned attempt to become drug free.

Most methadone withdrawal symptoms are:
- A planned part of a clear intention to become drug free
- At the end of a planned detox with an intention to give up drug use
- Experienced without the relieving effects of concurrent drug use.

These factors probably all increase the stress associated with methadone dose reductions and serve to increase the subjective experience of withdrawal symptoms. Discussion of these issues with the client will probably serve to reduce the severity of the withdrawal experience.

Follow up/relapse prevention

People who have been using opiates for some time and who detoxify using methadone often benefit from support and assistance for some time afterwards. Plans and support mechanisms for the period after the detox should be in place before it commences.

Risk of relapse is always high as there are many potential causes of relapse including:
- Protracted withdrawal symptoms
- Insomnia
- Environmental cues
- Contact with current users
- Stress
- Anxiety
- Low self esteem
- Depression.

The person who has succeeded in getting off opiates will need help to resist these cues to relapse. Often clients are reluctant to return to prescribing services for follow-up support and there are often few services for those that do.

Support that would help and could be provided by drug services includes:
- 'Coming off/staying off' therapeutic groups
- Relapse prevention training
- Individual counselling
- Self help groups
- Life skills instruction, assertiveness, etc.
- Naltrexone treatment.

Support that could be suggested/facilitated by drug services includes:
- Careers advice
- Further education
- Narcotics Anonymous meetings
- Vocational training.

summary

■ The physical process of detoxification is, in itself, relatively easy to achieve.

■ Long-term abstinence from opiate use is much harder to achieve.

■ Most opiate users will undergo detoxification many times before they achieve lasting periods opiate free.

■ Prescribed medication to assist in these detoxes will probably be a feature on more than one occasion.

■ Lofexidine is a useful non-opiate treatment for both community and in-patient rapid detoxification.

■ It is important that services respond to the requests for help in a therapeutic way that reduces drug-related harm and helps the client move on and learn from their experiences.

■ Drug users who become abstinent are vulnerable to relapse.

■ Drug services should offer full support for at least 6 months following detox.

section 10

Practical issues in methadone prescribing

Confidentiality	**130**
Clients going away	**130**
Contracting	**131**
Urinalysis	**132**
Typical drug clearance times	**134**
Hair analysis	**134**
'Manipulation'	**136**
Terminating treatment	**136**
Benzodiazepines	**137**
Recreational drug use	**138**
Problem alcohol use	**138**
Worker supervision and support	**138**
Transfer from injectable to oral methadone	**139**
Summary	**140**

Introduction

This section covers some of the areas of methadone prescribing that all workers and services need to consider carefully. Preparation of policies and strategies to deal with these practical issues will greatly assist in the smooth and effective running of any prescribing service.

Confidentiality

There are a number of reasons why drug users may be anxious about people finding out about their opiate use which may include some or all of the list below.

Opiate users are often:
- Held in very low regard
- Worried by guilt feelings about their drug use
- Anxious because they have not told key professionals about their drug use before e.g. health visitor, GP or probation officer
- Aware that some professionals still believe that a heroin-using parent is a bad parent
- Concerned that friends and relatives will react to them differently if they find out about their opiate use.

These concerns and the level of anxiety are added to by the fact that:
- Heroin use is illegal.

For these reasons it is important to be clear with drug users about who will become aware of their methadone treatment. If information is to be passed on then the method and content of the disclosure needs to be explained clearly.

Fears about the lack of confidentiality within the NHS and other drug services is one of the areas cited by clients who are not in contact with services as a reason for not making contact. Being explicit with all clients about what confidentiality means to you and your agency will help reduce paranoia and anxiety among both the group who are in contact with your service and those who are not.

Clients going away

The practicalities of picking up a methadone prescription from the prescribing doctor and/ or collecting the methadone itself can be restricting. Clients wanting to go away and requesting changes to their prescribing regime to accommodate this can be a major cause of friction. For this reason it is good practice to include a clause in the prescribing agreement that details how much notice is required for changes to be made in the regime and, if possible, what the parameters will be around accommodating employment or holidays.

If the client is leaving the country they may need an export licence: see Section 5: Methadone and the law.

As with all other aspects of prescribing it is important to weigh any possible risks – particularly those of overdose and illicit sale of methadone – against the therapeutic advantages of work or holiday.

Other possibilities for retaining some degree of control while allowing the travel or work plans to proceed are:
- Finding a pharmacy near the destination and arranging to post the methadone prescription there
- Arranging a temporary prescription with a doctor or prescribing service near the destination
- Checking with the local pharmacies and arranging evening methadone pick-ups.

However, in the end, it is important for the prescribing doctor not to feel pressured into making prescribing arrangements that may not be safe, and for the client to realise that sufficient warning must be given and that some negotiation has to take place before prescribing arrangements can be altered.

Contracting

The prescribing contract is not simply a set of rules the client must obey. Rather it is an agreement in which the client agrees to work with the prescribing service and in return the service agrees to prescribe methadone and provide an agreed level of support and help.

It should be borne in mind that there are few other areas of health care which require people to enter into contracts. A badly written contract that is simply a list of rules the client must obey can leave the client feeling devalued. Contracts should include the complaint procedures available to the client should they be dissatisfied with the service they receive.

It is important to read the contract to each client and discuss each issue in detail, not least because they may have literacy problems which they are reluctant to disclose.

In drawing up a contract it is important that if cessation of prescribing is mentioned as a response to behaviour, it is in terms that allow a measure of discretion or it is used only in circumstances in which there would be no doubt about the decision to stop prescribing.

This is particularly important with regard to clauses about illicit drug use as you may not want to respond to increases in drug taking and HIV risk behaviour by withdrawing treatment.

Components of a prescribing contract

The contract is usually between the prescribing doctor, client and drug worker.

The agreement should include what each party agrees to do, which in most cases would include the doctor agreeing to:
■ Provide a regular methadone prescription
■ Liaise with the drug worker regarding the client's progress
■ Discuss alterations in the agreed prescribing regime with the drug worker and client

The drug worker agreeing to:
■ See the client at agreed intervals
■ Be available within an agreed time should the client request extra time
■ Liaise with the prescribing doctor
■ Review the programme with the client and doctor at agreed intervals

The client agreeing to:
■ Attend appointments with the drug worker and doctor
■ Accept full responsibility for the perscription and medication once issued
■ Give adequate warning of plans to go away/request alterations to the prescribing regime
■ Provide urine samples for drug screen when requested
■ Reduce and minimise use of illicit drugs and to try and stop heroin use
■ Use methadone for personal use and not sell or share any of the prescription
■ Not to approach any other doctor for psychiatric medication during the treatment programme

And all parties agreeing that:
■ They will not use abusive or threatening behaviour
■ Any breach of the agreement will result in a review of the programme
■ A serious breach may result in termination of the prescription regime.

Urinalysis

A urine drug screen that is opiate positive is an essential safeguard that should always be obtained at the outset of treatment. However, it is easy to over-emphasise the importance of urinalysis in methadone treatment. It cannot give a full picture of someone's drug use (unless it is done daily – which is prohibitively expensive). It can only ever give a snapshot indication of drug use. It carries with it a number of dangers to the relationship between the prescriber/drug worker and client.[91]

The testing procedure
The urine specimen can be collected in a standard sterile pathology lab bottle and labelled accurately in the presence of the client.

The pathology lab form can be filled in by anyone but, unless there are special arrangements, must be signed by a doctor. The form would normally state: 'receiving methadone treatment, full drug screen please' although some services specify the drugs they want screened for e.g. '...please screen for methadone and other opiates, cocaine and amphetamine'.

The urine sample should be:
- Kept in the dark
- Refrigerated
- Tested as soon as possible.

The tests used
Most laboratories will use a relatively insensitive test first of all and, where a trace of a drug is found, follow it up with a more accurate test to confirm.

If this procedure is used it is unlikely that there would be a false positive result for methadone (or any other drug) although there is a possibility of a false negative result. This is particularly likely if the client has added water to the sample or drunk large quantities of fluid to reduce the concentration of illicit drugs in the urine.

The tests used are:
- Thin layer chromatography
- Paper chromatography
- Gas chromatography
- EMIT scan.

The benefits of urinalysis
Urinalysis is used as part of methadone treatment to:
- Confirm heroin use prior to treatment commencing

and, once treatment has commenced, to:
- Confirm methadone is being taken
- Discourage illicit/additional drug use
- Assess illicit/additional drug use
- Inform treatment decisions such as allowing take-home doses, dose increases and reductions and removal from programmes
- Provide information to support research into prescribing programmes.

The value of urinalysis in these functions is largely unresearched and, in some respects, a flawed procedure. Its use in each of these functions is outlined below.

Urinalysis prior to treatment
A urine test prior to commencement of treatment is a standard feature of almost all methadone prescribing. It is a useful safeguard against accusations of irresponsible prescribing as it is good evidence of opiate use prior to commencement of treatment.

However it is only evidence of at least one dose of a drug having been taken in the last 24–72 hours: see the drug clearance times chart below. It gives no indication as to the quantity of drugs being used nor evidence as to how long the client has been using those drugs. And as it is widely known among drug users that a urine screen for drugs will be part of the assessment procedure they will generally ensure that the result is 'opiate positive'.

The taking of a urine sample as part of the assessment procedure can easily convey to the client a message of distrust. It is therefore important to stress its role as a safeguard for the prescribing programme and as corroboration of the history given at assessment, rather than as a way of catching people out.

Confirming that methadone is being taken

This is an important part of the reason for testing urine for clients who can take their methadone home, and again forms useful documentary evidence against accusations of irresponsible prescribing.

Because methadone is a long-acting drug which is metabolised over a period of days, false negative urine screens are rare in clients who are taking their medication regularly – and should therefore be taken seriously and repeated as a further safeguard.

Confirmation that methadone is being taken requires a sample to be positive for both methadone and methadone metabolites.

Discouraging illicit/additional drug use

The extent to which the drug screening of urine samples deters illicit drug use is debatable, especially if the clients can predict when they are likely to be tested.

Although there are individual cases in which urinalysis can be helpful the extensive literature search carried out by Ward *et al*[91] failed to find any studies that could demonstrate a reliable link between urinalysis (as part of a methadone maintenance programme) and reduced illicit drug use.

Assessing illicit/additional drug use

However if someone can stop using for a few days prior to urine tests on a regular basis then they probably have a degree of control over their drug use. The issues around occasional drug use can therefore be addressed and systems that rely on urinalysis alone may miss this altogether.

If the client cannot stop using other drugs, even when they know a urine test is imminent, it is likely that they have not got much control over their drug use and this is an issue which needs addressing.

Informing treatment decisions

Urine screen results are commonly used to inform clinical decisions such as:

- Allowing take-home doses
- Increasing or decreasing the number of days' take-home doses allowed
- Dose increases
- Dose reductions
- Removal from prescribing programmes.

However it is important that if a drug screen result is to be used in clinical decision making it is not the only indicator that is used.

Providing information to support research into prescribing programmes

Urine testing can give an indication for research purposes as to the illicit drug use of people receiving methadone, although its limitations (see above) mean that it is difficult to produce methodologically-sound conclusions on the basis of drug screening the urine of clients.

Because of this the interpretation of results may well depend on whether the reader is a drug user, drug worker, doctor, service funder, politician or researcher and whether or not they are hostile to or supportive of prescribing services.

Drawbacks of urinalysis

The research that has been carried out into the efficacy of urine testing has been unable to demonstrate that it is a reliably effective way of monitoring drug use. A therapeutic, open and trusting relationship in which the client is not afraid to disclose the true picture of their drug use is likely to produce a more accurate and productive indication of drug-using patterns.[90] However used in conjunction with a therapeutic relationship, psychological and other treatments, urinalysis may be useful in encouraging clients to meet appropriate goals related to controlling and reducing their illicit drug use.

The experience of many workers is that the more heavily methadone prescribing is policed, and the more the feeling of 'them and us' grows, the more ingenious the dodges become to avoid getting caught.

The 'them and us' syndrome can be countered through careful explanation of the test and the rationale for it. Most clients accept that some people are motivated to get methadone simply to sell it and that it is legitimate for services to use objective measures from time to time to check that they are providing an appropriate service. Clients also accept that many seek treatment to maximise drug consumption and that workers need objective tools to help determine what the real patterns of drug use are.

There are a number of ways clients can avoid getting a urinalysis result that is unfavourable, such as:
■ Bringing in someone else's urine in a small container kept under the arm (to keep it warm)
■ Getting someone else in the toilets to provide a sample
■ Adding water to the sample to dilute any unwanted metabolites.

The only reliable way of avoiding these is to supervise the production of the sample. This is a demeaning procedure for both client and staff member. However if the benefits are clear it may be worth while.

Typical drug clearance times

There is room on the chart below for you to fill in the values your pathology lab gives you according to the tests they perform, although they are unlikely to be much different from the values given.

Always remember that drug clearance times vary according to the:
■ Dose of the drug taken
■ Sensitivity of the tests used
■ Ph value of the urine: more acidic urine tends to produce shorter clearance times
■ Combination of drugs used: for instance stimulants increase the metabolic rate and therefore reduce drug clearance times.

Hair analysis

The hair can act as a 'chemical tape recorder', providing a record of drugs taken. It can be analysed centimetre by centimetre giving a clear picture of drug use over a period of months.

Hair analysis is commercially available in the UK. For most services it will complement rather than compete with urinalysis as it is rather expensive for routine use.

It is particularly valuable in:
■ Monitoring people who are stable on methadone maintenance and who are seen only occasionally
■ Assessing patients whose drug-using history is doubtful
■ Monitoring levels of drug use over the long term.

Drug clearance times chart

Drug	Time after which a urine screen will show negative
Methadone	2–4 days
Heroin	1–2 days
Diazepam and other benzodiazepines	2–4 days
Cocaine	1–2 days
Amphetamine	1–2 days
MDMA (ecstasy)	2–4 days
LSD	1–3 days
Cannabis	4–28 days

Pros and cons of urine and hair analysis

Urinalysis	Hair analysis
Open to deception and evasion	Deception proof (but clients can present with all their hair cut off!)
Supervising sample production is demeaning	Civilised procedure
Indicates drug use over past few days	Indicates drug use over past few months, month by month
Insensitive to low levels of use	Sensitive to low levels of use
Insensitive to occasional use	Sensitive to occasional use
Qualitative	Quantitative – allows comparison of drug use month by month
Tester potentially at risk of infection	No risk of infection
Results can be accessed quickly	Delayed results
Inexpensive	Expensive

'Manipulation'

The history of drug users being seen as manipulative by health professionals is rooted in past conflicts between drug users and the medical establishment over drugs. For a long time doctors have had control over the commodity that can be the single most important thing in the life of a drug user. Society's strong disapproval of the non-medical use of certain drugs, coupled with the historical desire of doctors to retain control of supply, has meant that control has been very tight.

Everyone who wants something will try different stratagems in order to get it – and the more they want it the more inventive they are inclined to be in the devices they employ. Furthermore if a strategy (however socially unacceptable) has worked once it is likely to be repeated.

It is not so long since the only way any doctor could be persuaded to write an opiate prescription for an 'addict' was if s/he was made to believe that the person genuinely wanted to give up drug use forever, and that the only thing that would help was a detoxification to help with the initial withdrawals. Clearly in these circumstances anyone who wanted a prescription, regardless of their true intentions, knew that their only hope was to spin the old 'I want to get off' yarn. The failure of these 'detoxes' has been a formative experience for many doctors.

With the advent of more flexible prescribing this problem has been reduced. Most drug services have found that any increase in flexibility and understanding is met with a corresponding reduction in 'manipulative' strategies to obtain the desired treatment.

The limit to flexibility is that the prescribing must not increase drug-related harm. Drug users may still employ techniques to persuade the providers of treatment to do things that will not be helpful to them.

However opportunities for manipulation with its resulting friction and dissatisfaction will be minimised if we:
■ Are clear and realistic about our treatment aims
■ Communicate effectively with our colleagues
■ Have clear written agreements with our clients
■ Encourage our clients to have an overt agenda
■ Try and offer appropriate and effective treatment.

Terminating treatment

Methadone is not a treatment that works for everyone. In addition to people who are too chaotic in their drug use to meet the requirements made by prescribing programmes there will always be the occasional person succeeding in getting a methadone prescription who:
■ Is not suited for treatment
■ Convinces the assessor to prescribe more methadone than is necessary
■ Gives a fictitious history to receive an inappropriate treatment duration
■ Is unable to achieve any of the treatment goals.

It is often easier to identify these clients after they have been started on a prescribing programme rather than before and the review procedures should take this into account.

Treatment may be terminated if:
■ It is doing more harm than good – with no prospect of this changing
■ There has been a serious breach of contract e.g. violence towards staff
■ There have been repeated breaches of contract e.g. non attendance at appointments.

Termination of treatment is a serious step, especially if there may be a return to high-risk behaviours as a result. Prescribing staff must be certain that it is a necessary intervention.

It is important that the criteria for removal from methadone prescribing are understood by all concerned and that they are applied fairly and without discrimination. Where possible clients should receive verbal and written warnings prior to removal from treatment. Other options that fall short of permanent removal, such as suspension of prescribing, may be considered.

Where possible entry criteria for returning to methadone treatment, including the earliest date a referral will be considered, should be made clear to the client.

Benzodiazepines

Use of benzodiazepines is, for many heroin users, part of the opiate-using culture. They are seen as relatively benign drugs that can be taken without withdrawal effects. This may be because benzodiazepine withdrawals could be mistaken for opiate withdrawals.

Benzodiazepines are sometimes used by opiate users to help them sleep, although often in doses far in excess of the normal therapeutic range. They are also used during the day when the user has no intention of sleeping to achieve the following effects:
■ Creating a feeling of not being part of the rest of the world
■ Causing complete amnesia of the time spent intoxicated
■ Increased confidence
■ Feeling 'drunk'
■ Potentiating the effects of alcohol
■ Reducing the severity of opiate withdrawal symptoms.

The relationship between benzodiazepines and methadone is twofold:
■ Requests for methadone prescription are frequently accompanied by a request for a concurrent benzodiazepine prescription
■ People on methadone will often continue to use illicit benzodiazepines when they have stopped using illicit opiates.

The main problems are that:
■ The therapeutic value of benzodiazepines in terms of sleep promotion is lost after only 2–4 weeks of treatment
■ When taken in excess they can cause chaotic, high-risk behaviour with memory loss of events while intoxicated
■ Their use contributes to higher levels of HIV/hepatitis risk behaviour
■ The withdrawal syndrome – which includes agoraphobia and panic attacks – can be distressing and trigger further drug use.

As they are not controlled drugs it may not be possible for services to arrange dispensing of any less than a week's supply at a time - and there is often a high risk of them all being consumed in the first 24 hour period. It is therefore difficult to prescribe benzodiazepines using the rationale of harm reduction.

Methadone prescribing services that operate a non-benzodiazepine prescribing policy may:
■ Be at less risk from accusations of irresponsible prescribing
■ Reduce requests for benzodiazepines
■ Promote discussion and insight into benzodiazepine use

but they will not meet the needs of people with genuine benzodiazepine dependency or be able to take advantage of the short-term therapeutic benefits when their use is clinically indicated.

Many clients are willing to 'trade' their benzodiazepine request for extra methadone. A regime of 5mg methadone for 10mg temazepam/5mg diazepam to a maximum of 25% above the assessed methadone need, based on opiate use alone, is used by some services. This is not always appropriate and is thought by some to be flawed in terms of logic, especially as methadone will have little or no effect on benzodiazepine withdrawals. Some services offer a diazepam detox running alongside methadone treatment for the first few weeks to give people a realistic chance of coming off.

If a client remains adamant that they need prescribed benzodiazepines it is reasonable to start the methadone prescribing and to require them to remain in treatment for a period of extended assessment prior to a decision being made on prescribing benzodiazepines.

Recreational drug use

Most people on methadone prescriptions continue to take other drugs in addition to their methadone, particularly cannabis.

The test which needs to be applied is not that of abstinence but rather of the treatment aims. If the additional drug use is not compromising the treatment aims then it should not jeopardise the continuation of prescribing. If it is threatening the treatment aims then the care plan may need to be adjusted in order to achieve those aims before termination of treatment is considered. Problematic additional opiate use is discussed in the next section: Prescribing for groups with special needs: People who 'use on top'.

It is important that prescribing services are clear among themselves and with clients on what the treatment aims are and what the response will be to recreational drug use.

Problem alcohol use

A significant minority of people on methadone prescriptions have a concurrent alcohol dependence. Alcohol and methadone potentiate each other and thus the risks of overdose are greatly increased when people are drinking heavily in addition to using methadone. Alcohol is thought to be a contributing factor in many of the methadone overdoses.

Some clients alternate between opiates and alcohol and for these people methadone is often helpful because while on methadone alcohol consumption falls or stops. It is those who have a dual dependency that present the biggest problems to prescribing services.

Additional services that may be offered to reduce risk and increase appropriateness of treatment include:
- Supervised consumption of methadone
- Breathalysing prior to dispensing of methadone
- Hospital or community alcohol detoxification prior to commencement of (or during) methadone treatment
- Liver function tests and other health investigations
- Concurrent dispensing of disulfiram (Antabuse) – started in hospital to reduce risks
- Discussion of alcohol consumption as a specific item on the care plan
- Residential rehabilitation.

Worker supervision and support

Clinical supervision is a key issue in providing effective methadone prescribing services. Opiate users present in many different ways and present unique challenges in the needs they have.

In order to offer an equitable, consistent and sustainable service clinicians must have access to supervision which allows them to discuss both the clinical and personal issues that are raised for them in their work.

Clinicians involved in working with opiate users also benefit from the support and opportunities to develop practice through:
- Conferences
- Regional drug workers fora
- Special interest groups
- Journal clubs
- Specialist training.

Transfer from injectable to oral methadone

There are a number of reasons why both the clinician and the client may want to transfer from a prescription of oral and injectable methadone to oral only. These include:

■ Vein damage being exacerbated by continued injection

■ A desire to move away from illicit drug-using patterns

■ Pressure from partner or family

■ Recognition that stopping injecting is a precondition to successful detox

■ Agency or purchaser policy requires everyone on methadone treatment to receive oral methadone.

The transfer from injectable to oral methadone can be a very difficult and slow process which is one of the reasons many services choose not to prescribe injectables and instead try and stabilise clients on oral methadone from the start.

The process is one of a negotiated reduction in the injectable portion of the prescription and a simultaneous increase in the oral portion. Sometimes this process can be made easier by increasing the oral portion of the prescription by a little more than the reduction in the injectable methadone. For instance a client on 1x10mg ampoule per day may be given an extra 15–20mg oral methadone to replace it.

During this process it is important to check injecting sites regularly and encourage the client to use counselling and psychological support services.

Sometimes, as with detox, the best approach is to agree with the client prior to any changes that the process is an experiment, with the option to return to the original dose/route remaining open. This removes the pressure on both worker and client to see the process in terms of sucess or failure and for clients to resist change for fear they might be giving something up forever.

The transfer is more likely to be successful (in terms of avoiding a relapse to injecting illicit drugs) if it takes place in gradual steps. For people with a long history of injecting, full transfer to oral medication can take up to two years. Towards the end of the process, when nearly all the ampoules have been 'converted' into oral methadone, the client may continue to have one injecting day per script cycle, and this final phase can be the longest. Relapses need to be expected and dealt with as learning experiences.

summary

- Many of the commonly experienced problems in methadone prescribing can be reduced by open, honest relationships and written contracts.

- Responsible use of urinalysis seeks to strike a balance in which the urine test is a positive corroboration for the written records of information given to the worker.

- Urinalysis has an important role in providing documentary evidence to support methadone prescribing at the start of treatment.

- The limitations mean that only limited weight should be given to the result of the initial urinalysis.

- Prescribing benzodiazepines to opiate users should only be undertaken by specialist prescribers, within clear guidelines.

- Problem alcohol use may contra-indicate methadone prescribing.

section 11

Prescribing for

groups with

special needs

Pregnant women	**142**
Babies withdrawing from opiates	**143**
Young people	**144**
Clients with responsibility for young people	**145**
People who have HIV	**145**
Minority ethnic groups	**146**
People who 'use on top'	**146**
People who 'don't get better'	**147**
People with mental health problems	**147**
People dependent on injection practice	**148**
Summary	**149**

Introduction

Although the majority of people who are prescribed methadone are white Anglo-Saxon males between 25 and 40 years old, they are not a homogenous group with the same needs nor are they the only group who receive or need methadone treatment. This section looks at the groups of clients with special needs who use, or could benefit from, but avoid, methadone prescribing services.

Pregnant women

Guilt and anxiety are often features of pregnancy in opiate-using women. People often assume that opiates and methadone in themselves will cause congenital abnormalities in the foetus. However there is no evidence to support this assertion. A booklet called *Drugs, Pregnancy and Childcare*, published in 1992 by ISDD and available direct from them, is useful further reading.

For a full discussion of the effects of methadone on the foetus see Section 4: Physiology and pharmacology of methadone.

The risks to the mother and baby that services can have some influence over are:
- Lack of ante-natal care
- Maternal withdrawal syndrome triggering premature labour
- Multiple drug use which includes drugs which can cause damage to the foetus (such as alcohol)
- Fatal overdose from injected illicit heroin
- Infection through unsafe injection practices
- Poor nutrition
- Smoking tobacco
- Sudden cessation of methadone treatment.

Interagency co-operation

Pregnant opiate-using women should be assessed by a drugs worker, in addition to medical and midwife assessment.

Where necessary interagency co-operation should help ensure that the mother receives the best possible care and treatment.

The following liaison procedure has been suggested as good practice.[92] However its potential for raising anxieties unnecessarily should be recognised. The aim should be for as normal a pregnancy and birth as possible, and in the absence of concern about the safety of the child or mother, it is often sufficient for the prescriber or drug service to liaise with the GP, community midwife and health visitor, and with the hospital.

Procedure where there is concern

A 'booking meeting' should be held after pregnancy is confirmed which involves all the workers concerned and the mother (and partner or significant other). The presence of a nominated obstetrician and a member of the maternity unit staff can help allay any anxieties of the staff, as well as that of the client, that she will not receive sufficient analgesia.

The purpose of this meeting is to:
- Identify pre-birth key worker
- Share information
- Discuss drug treatment options (see below)
- Decide on whether or not a child protection case conference needs to be held.

A second meeting of the same staff should be planned for 2 weeks before the expected date of delivery. The possibility of premature labour must be considered and the date of this meeting brought forward, if necessary. The purpose of this meeting is to:
- Share the key worker's current assessment
- Discuss long and short-term plans
- Decide whether a child protection case conference needs to be held prior to discharge.

Following the birth there should be a pre-discharge meeting with membership as above and including a paediatrician to:
■ Assess bonding and parenting
■ Ensure that appropriate care will be provided in the community
■ Confirm the identity of the key worker
■ Decide whether a review meeting will be needed at 3 months.

The purpose of the review meeting at 3 months is:
■ Formal feedback and liaison.

Methadone treatment in pregnancy

The methadone treatment of choice with a pregnant woman is often thought to be detoxification. However this is not always the case. In particular withdrawal symptoms should be avoided in the first 3 months of pregnancy because of the increased risk of miscarriage. Withdrawal symptoms can also induce premature labour during the last 3 months of pregnancy.

Pregnancy is a time when many women are able to make changes such as giving up drugs because of the added motivation of being pregnant. Where this is possible it should be encouraged and supported by the workers involved.

However many women find that during pregnancy they experience an increase in:
■ Stress
■ Pressure from family, friends, drug users and drug workers
■ Feelings of inability to cope and lack of control over life
– all of which can lead to increased drug use.

Skilled, careful and non-judgmental assessment of the situation is therefore essential prior to a treatment plan being formulated.

If detoxification is chosen it is important that contingency plans are made for the prevention and management of relapse following the birth.

The optimal time to detox is the second 3-month period of the pregnancy. The normal maximum reduction in the daily dose in any week is 10mg. The final, slower part of a detox is often carried out (under close medical supervision) in the final 3 months of pregnancy without risk to the baby.

However only a proportion of women will be able to achieve abstinence because of either relapse or obstetric complications. Short or long-term methadone maintenance will be the treatment chosen by most pregnant women.[91]

As what is best for the mother is best for the foetus the dose should be adequate to enable the mother to avoid illicit heroin use.

Babies withdrawing from opiates

Care of the withdrawing infant

Although one study found it to be ineffective, a quiet, darkened room and close wrapping may calm the baby and remove the need for drug treatment. Babies can usually be cared for in the normal maternity environment provided they can be moved to special care units if necessary.

In the UK, if treatment is required, chlorpromazine is usually used with a regime such as the following:
■ Chlorpromazine 1–3mg/Kg/24 hours in 4 divided doses for 5–10 days then gradual withdrawal over 14–21 days.

The literature also includes withdrawal regimes using other non-opioid drugs such as phenobarbitone, clonidine and the benzodiazepine diazepam, opiate drugs such as camphorated opium tincture (Paregoric) and methadone.

Breast-feeding

There is no conclusive evidence about how much, or indeed whether, methadone passes from mother to baby in breast-feeding. If there is transfer of methadone the doses will be very low. Therefore the general advantages of breast-feeding, and the fact that if it is passed to the baby it may help to reduce any withdrawals, mean that breast-feeding can be encouraged.

Care of the parents of a withdrawing infant

Most mothers of babies who suffer opiate withdrawals feel very guilty and therefore censure from staff is unlikely to be a helpful intervention.

It is important for staff to deal with their feelings about a mother's drug use separately from their care of her and the baby – especially if the mother requires extra help in learning to care for her child. Drug service staff can often be of assistance in the process of helping maternity staff understand the drug-related issues and their feelings towards drug-using mothers.

The rationale for prescribing to the baby should be explained to the parents. It may be necessary to tell parents that they must never administer opiates to the child – even if it displays distress similar to withdrawal symptoms.

If admission to a special care baby unit is required it is helpful for the parents to be introduced to the staff as soon as possible.

Young people

The Children Act 1989

The Children Act enshrined in law the principle that in all care the interests of the child are paramount. This means that a worker has a responsibility to inform the appropriate authorities if they believe a young person (whether directly their client or not) may be at serious risk from any of the following:
- Physical harm
- Psychological harm
- Sexual harm
- Neglect.

This will usually be the line manager in the first instance and then social services.
It is not possible for workers to argue that the drug user, not the child, is their client and that therefore they should do nothing, or that it is the responsibility of other workers to identify these issues.

Because of this it is good practice for workers to explain to the client at the outset their responsibilities with regard to confidentiality and child protection. It is useful to explain to clients what 'serious harm' means as well as informing them of the factors that might cause concern regarding care of a child. However this must be done sensitively and the client must be reassured that 'at risk' is not synonymous with 'in the care of a parent who is prescribed methadone'.

Methadone treatment for young people

Methadone is unlikely to be an appropriate treatment for young people (usually taken to mean under 16s – but possibly including immature 17 year olds) because they are unlikely to have:
- Long-term opiate use
- Significant tolerance
- Heroin using problems that are not amenable to other forms of help and treatment.

Parental consent to treatment will almost always be required. If a skilled assessment has ascertained that the young person is mature enough to be able to give informed consent to treatment, the Scarman ruling in the Victoria Gillick case would appear to make treatment without parental consent a legal option. In such cases the whole decision – making process needs to be very carefully documented.

In-patient assessment and specialist consultant prescribing are strongly indicated if methadone treatment is considered for a young person.

Clients with responsibility for young people

The vast majority of drug users do take adequate care of their children and drug use alone is not necessarily a cause for concern and is certainly not reason enough to initiate care proceedings.

If the client has responsibility for children the Children Act 1989 is clear that as far as the worker is concerned the needs of the child are paramount.

If it appears that there are times when there are no suitable arrangements for the care of children who are at risk of serious physical, psychological or emotional harm or at risk through neglect, a skilled and full assessment should be carried out. The local authority has a responsibility to offer help and support to the parents or carers and child. This must be done sensitively and with the long-term aim of helping the family stay together where this is in the best interests of the child.

It is important that people working with parents or carers understand the Children Act and have immediate access to supervision and specialist social work support if child care becomes an issue.

People who have HIV

Methadone treatment can reduce behaviours which compromise the immune system such as injecting, and can reduce stress and improve diet and other factors which are likely to accelerate the progression of HIV disease.

In prescribing methadone for clients who have HIV it is important to:
- Encourage a multi-agency approach to treatment of symptomatic HIV infection
- Discuss hepatitis B and/or C infection with the client as they are more likely to have these infections as well
- Maintain close liaison with the client's HIV physician and be aware of the other services involved in providing care
- Observe for reducing tolerance to methadone during periods of illness and weight loss
- Ensure that if the client has memory loss they are not at risk from accidental overdose through forgetting they have taken the medication
- Ensure that the client fully understands transmission routes.

Only prescribe drugs for the treatment of HIV-related illness as a last resort if the client refuses to see a specialist doctor. Prescribing treatment for symptomatic HIV is best done in conjunction with a specialist, as methadone interactions with drugs used in the treatment of HIV such as AZT, are not yet fully researched or understood.

Drug users who have had a positive HIV test will have a variety of responses and needs. A positive test in itself may not change drug-using behaviour. Although for some it will lead to positive changes for others it may trigger a period of chaotic drug use.

The process of adjusting to living with HIV may involve not only coming to terms with feelings of loss and grief but also a discovery of life or rediscovery of a purpose to live, in the knowledge that they cannot become uninfected.

Treatment options are the same for opiate users, regardless of HIV status, and a full assessment needs to be carried out to weigh up the pros and cons of the available treatments.

Some drug users who are living with HIV may avoid dealing with the many feelings they experience by using prescribed and illicit drugs in a dangerous and chaotic way. This can be exacerbated by the knowledge that as there are serious health consequences in being discharged from a methadone prescribing programme, termination of the prescription may be less likely, possibly leading to disruptive behaviour and refusal to comply with the prescribing contract.

Minority ethnic groups

Traditionally drug services have been managed, staffed and run overwhelmingly by and for the white population. There is often a perception among ethnic groups that the services are not for them.

It is incumbent upon services not only to have equal opportunities policies and to employ staff from ethnic backgrounds but also to offer culturally appropriate services to ethnic communities as a whole, and to the drug users within those communities.

People who 'use on top'

Most opiate users continue to use cannabis in addition to their methadone prescription and where this is not interfering with the primary treatment aims it is tolerated by most drug services.

Clearly in order to be able to deal with additional drug use the worker must first be aware of it. This means either forming a therapeutic relationship with the client in which these issues can be discussed (which will normally mean that the threat of removal

of prescribing on discovery of illicit drug use is not a useful part of the agreement) or having effective urine screening procedures which, as discussed in Section 10, is difficult and expensive.

It is important to assess the scale, nature and motivation of illicit drug use before taking action. There is a world of difference between using heroin every other 'giro day' and using it on a daily basis, and frequently selling the methadone, and while the latter may require action the former may be enough of an improvement to continue with no change to the programme.

People take heroin in addition to their methadone for a number of reasons which include:
■ It 'feels better' to take heroin than methadone
■ They enjoy feeling out of control
■ They are experiencing withdrawal symptoms
■ Their partner is using heroin
■ They find injecting a ritual that is difficult to live without
■ They believe that recreational heroin use is possible and relatively harmless
■ As a way of coping with problems
■ They have used up the take-home dose of methadone.

If it is identified that illicit drug use is occurring and jeopardising the treatment aims appropriate strategies should be employed to reduce risk behaviour.

Treatment options include increasing:
■ Daily methadone dose
■ Frequency of methadone collection
■ Supervised consumption
■ Time spent with the client by counselling staff

and:
■ Appropriate offers of 'rewards' following achievement of realistic treatment goals
■ Drug-free residential rehabilitation
■ Suspension of prescribing.

People who 'don't get better'

Frustration at the 'failure' of opiate users to 'recover' and become drug-free quickly following efforts to help them is a feeling experienced by many workers. The answer to this feeling of frustration usually lies in reducing expectations rather than increasing pressure on the client to 'do better'.

Opiate dependence, once established, is a long-term problem characterised by:

■ The desire to take opiates as a central part of life
■ Tolerance of many adverse consequences of drug use
■ Long periods of time spent contemplating change
■ Periods of greater and lesser use
■ Periods of abstinence followed by relapse.

Towards the end of an 'opiate-using career' these periods of abstinence usually become longer and the periods of relapse shorter.

Demoralising the client by constantly admonishing their failures is unlikely to help them move forward or use help constructively. An approach which recognises where the client is, sets appropriate goals, and offers appropriate help will be more successful.

People with mental health problems

Prevalence of some mental health problems has been found to be significantly higher in opiate users than in the general population.[91] For many of these people opiates may be a way of self-medicating the feelings caused by their mental health problems.

Rates of depression in opiate users have been found to be five times higher than in the general population.[94]

Careful history taking at initial assessment will pick up whether there is an increased likelihood of mental health problems and careful monitoring, particularly during detox, will detect the emergence of underlying mental health problems as the dose is reduced.

Most people who are being treated for mental health problems can be treated concurrently with methadone for their drug dependence. Some disorders such as depression and anxiety are likely to be improved by the increased stability and access to professional help afforded by methadone prescribing.

Some people use opiates as medication for paranoid or other psychotic ideas, and as such may become more ill as they stabilize or reduce their opiate intake.

Inappropriate referrals

Mental health services and other referring agencies may refer all clients with mental health problems and any history of drug use to the local drug service and expect them to deal with both. Liaison between drug and mental health services is vital in ensuring appropriate sharing of care for drug users with mental health problems.

People dependent on injection practice

Intravenous heroin users often change the frequency and level of risk of their injecting practice over time, and these changes may be encouraged or facilitated by drug services.[95]

For those clients who find injecting a powerful ritual, stopping altogether can be as hard to achieve as abstinence from drug use itself. Services must recognise that clients who achieve abstinence from compulsive injecting will feel frustration and support should be offered accordingly.

Reducing the harm associated with injecting may be helped by:
■ Working with the client to improve injection technique and reducing the frequency with which they inject
■ Higher doses of oral methadone
■ Prescribing injectable drugs
■ Discussing the rituals involved
■ Promoting insight into the motivations and triggers for injecting.

summary

■ Antenatal care should include input from a drug worker, and should aim to be as normal as possible.

■ Babies of opiate-using mothers can normally be cared for in the normal maternity environment.

■ The Children Act makes care of young people at risk a priority over all other considerations.

■ Parental drug use is not, in itself, sufficient cause for children to be placed on the register of children at risk.

■ Use of illicit opiates in addition to methadone should not normally lead to automatic removal from a methadone prescribing regime.

■ Problematic opiate use is often a long-term activity that is seldom quickly and completely resolved.

references

1   Gohdse H. (1989) *Drugs and Addictive Behaviour: A Guide to Treatment.* Chap.2. Blackwell Scientific Publications, Oxford.

2   Spear B. (1969) The growth of heroin addiction in the United Kingdom. *British Journal of Addiction*, **64**: 245.

3   Eichler O and Farah A. (1957) *Handbuch Der Experimentellen Pharmakologie.* Springer-Verlag, Berlin.

4   Bäumler E (1968) *A Century of Chemistry.* Econ Verlag, Dusseldorf.

5   Erhahart G and Ruschig H. (1972) *Arzneimittel Entwicklung Wirkung Darstellung*, Band 1, *Therapeutica mit Wirkung auf das Zentral Nervensystem.* Verlag Chemie, Weinheim.

6   Payte J T. (1991) A brief history of methadone in the treatment of opioid dependence: A personal perspective. *Journal of Psychoactive Drugs*, **23**: 103–7.

7   Bäumler E. (1992) *Die Grossen Medikamente.* Gustav Lübbe Verlag, Bergisch Gladbach.

8   Chen K K. (1948) *Pharmacology of methadone and related compounds.* Annals: New York Academy of Sciences.

9   May E L and Jacobson A E. (1989) The Committee on Problems of Drug Dependence: A legacy of the National Academy of Sciences. A historical account. *Drug and Alcohol Dependence*, **23**: 183–218.

10 Isbell H, Wikler A and Eddy N. (1947) Tolerance and addiction liability of 6-dimethylamino-4-4-diphenyl-heptanon-3 (methadon). *Journal of the American Medical Association*, **135**: 888–94.

11 Bockmühl M and Ehrhart G. (1949) Uber eine neue Klasse von spasmolytisch und analgetissch wirkenden Verindungen. *Justus Liebigs Ann. Chem.* **561:** 52.

12 Prescott F and Ransome S G. (1947) Amidone (miadone) as an obstetric analgesic, *Lancet* **2**: 501.

13 Duncan Mitchell, *Personal correspondence with the authors.* 31/1/95.

14 Edwards G and Busch C. (eds). (1981) *Drug problems in Britain: A review of 10 years*. Academic Press.

15 Stimson G V and Oppenheimer E. (1982) *Heroin addiction: Treatment and control in Britain.* Tavistock, London.

16 Hartnoll R L, Mitcheson M, Battersby A, *et al*. (1980) Evaluation of heroin maintenance in controlled trial. *Archives of General Psychiatry,* **37**:877–84.

17 Paxton R, Mullin P, and Beattie J. (1978) The effects of methadone maintenance with opioid takers: A review and findings from one British city. *British Journal of Psychiatry,* **132**: 473–81.

18 Home Office (1986) Statistics of drug addicts notified to the Home Office, United Kingdom, 1985. *Home Office Statistical Bulletin,* **40/86**. London, HMSO. Home Office (1994) Statistics of drug addicts notified to the Home Office, United Kingdom, 1993. *Home Office Statistical Bulletin,* **10/94** London, HMSO.

19 Advisory Council on the Misuse of Drugs. (1982)*Treatment and Rehabilitation Report*. HMSO, London.

20 Advisory Council on the Misuse of Drugs. (1988) *AIDS and Drug Misuse. Part 1.* HMSO, London.

21 Robertson J R, Bucknell A B V, Welsby P D, *et al*. (1986) Epidemic of AIDS-related virus (HTLV-III/LAV) infection among intravenous drug abusers. *British Medical Journal,* **292**: 527–30.

22 Hart G J, Sonnex C, Petherick A, *et al*. (1989) Risk behaviour for HIV infection amongst injecting drug users attending a drug dependency clinic. *British Medical Journal,* **298**: 1081–3.

23 Liappas J A, Jenner F A, and Vincente B. (1988) Literature on methadone maintenance clinics. *International Journal of Addiction*, **23**: 927–40.

24 Greenwood J. (1990) Creating a new drug service in Edinburgh. *British Medical Journal*, **300**: 587–9.

25 Dally A. (1987) Stabilise, not criminalise. *Druglink*, **Sep/Oct**: 14.

26 Dally A. (1990) *A doctor's story*. MacMillan. London.

27 Anon (1994) Conversation with Vincent Dole. *Addiction*, **89**: 23–9

28 Cooper J R. (1992) Ineffective use of psychoactive drugs: Methadone treatment is no exception. *Journal of the American Medical Association*, **267**: 281–2.

29 Ball J A and Ross A. (1991) *The effectiveness of methadone maintenance treatment*. Springer-Verlag, New York.

30 Strain E C, Stitzer M L, Liebson I A and Bigelow G E. (1993) Methadone dose and treatment outcome. *Drug and Alcohol Dependence*, **33**: 105–17.

31 Strain E C, Stitzer M L, Liebson I A and Bigelow G E. (1993) Dose-response effects of methadone in the treatment of opioid dependence. *Annals of Internal Medicine*, **119**: 23–7.

32 Hubbard R L, Marsden M E, Rachal J V, *et al*. (1989) *Drug Abuse Treatment: A National Study of Effectiveness*. University of North Carolina Press, Chapel Hill, NC.

33 Vogel V H, Isbell H and Chapman K W. Present status of narcotic addiction. *Journal of the American Medical Association*, **138**: 1019–26.

34 Kolb L and Himmelsbach C K. (1938) Clinical studies of drug addiction III. A critical review of the withdrawal treatments with method of evaluating abstinence syndromes. *Public Health Reports*, **128**: 1.

35 Gossop M. (1990) The development of a short opiate withdrawal scale (SOWS). *Addictive Behaviors*, **15**: 487–90.

36   Gossop M, Bradley M and Phillips G. (1987) An investigation of withdrawal symptoms shown by opiate addicts during and subsequent to a 21-day in-patient methadone detoxification procedure. *Addictive Behaviors* **12**: 1–6.

37   Phillips G, Gossop M and Bradley M. (1986) The influence of psychological factors on the opiate withdrawal syndrome. *British Journal of Psychiatry*, **149**: 235–8.

38   Green L and Gossop M. (1988) Effects of information on the opiate withdrawal syndrome. *British Journal of Addiction*, **83**: 305–9.

39   Gossop M, Griffiths P, Bradley M and Strang J. (1989) Opiate withdrawal symptoms in response to 10-day and 21-day methadone withdrawal programmes. *British Journal of Psychiatry*, **154**: 360–3.

40   Gossop M and Strang J. (1991) A comparison of the withdrawal responses of heroin and methadone addicts during detoxification. *British Journal of Psychiatry*, **158**: 697–9.

41   Gossop M, Johns A and Green L. (1986) Opiate withdrawal: In-patient versus out-patient programmes and preferred versus random assignment to treatment. *British Medical Journal*, **293**: 103–4.

42   Dawe S, Griffiths P, Gossop M and Strang J. (1991) Should opiate addicts be involved in controlling their own detoxification? A comparison of fixed vs. negotiable schedules. *British Journal of Addiction*, **86**: 977–82.

43   Yancovitz S R, Des Jarlais D C, Peyser N P, *et al.* (1991) A randomised trial of an interim methadone clinic. *American Journal of Public Health*, **81**: 1185–91.

44   Dole V P, Robinson J W, Orraca J, *et al* (1975) *New England Journal of Medicine*, **280**: 1372–5.

45   Newman R G, and Whitehill W B. (1979) Double-blind comparison of methadone and placebo maintenance treatments of narcotic addicts in Hong Kong. *Lancet*, **September 8**: 485–8.

46   Gunne L M and Gronbladh L (1981) The Swedish methadone maintenance program: A controlled study. *Drug and Alcohol Dependence*, **24**: 249–256.

47   Stitzer M L, Iguchi, M Y and Felch L J. (1992) Contingent take-home incentive: Effects on drug use of methadone maintenance patients. *Journal of Consulting and Clinical Psychology*, **60**: 927–34.

48   Ball J A and Ross A. (1991) *The effectiveness of methadone maintenance treatment*. Springer-Verlag, New York.

49   McLellan T A, Arndt I, Metzger D, *et al.* (1993) The effects of psychosocial services in substance abuse treatment. *Journal of the American Medical Association*, **269**: 1953–9.

50   Department of Health, Scottish Office Home & Health Dept, Welsh Office. (1991) *Drug Misuse and Dependence: Guidelines on clinical management*. HMSO, London.

51   Balzaar J. (1986) Formulation for extemporaneously prepared sugar free methadone mixture. *Pharm J*, **237**: 678.

52   Goodman O S. (ed). (1985) *The pharmacological basis of therapeutics.*, McMillan, New York, Chap. 22 by Jaffe J H and Martin W R.

53   Bozarth and Wize. (1984) quoted p499 in ref 72.

54   British National Formulary. (September 1989) **18**: 188.

55   Dollerey C Sir. (1991) *Therapeutic Drugs*. Churchill Livingstone, Edinburgh.

56   Cicero *et al.* (1975) Function of the male sex organs in heroin and methadone users. *New England Journal of Medicine*. **292**: 882–7

57   McCaul M E, Bigelow G, Stitzer M, *et al.* (1982) Short-term effects of oral methadone in methadone maintenence subjects. *Clin Journal Pharmacol. Theraputics*. **31(2)**: 753–61.

58   Dale A and Jones S S. (1992) *The Methadone Experience: the consumer view*. The Centre for Research, London.

59   Briggs G G, Freeman R K and Yaffe S J. (eds). *Drugs in pregnancy and lactation: a reference guide to foetal and neonatal risk*. 3rd Edition.

60   Johnstone F D, (1990) *Contemp. Rev. Obstet. Gynaecol.* **2**: May.

61   Newman R G, Bashkow S and Calko D. (1975) Results of 313 consecutive live births delivered to patients in the New York City methadone maintenence programme. *American Journal of Obstetrics and Gynaecology*, **121**: 233–7.

62   Naeye K L, Blanc W and Khatamee M A. Fetal complications of maternal heroin addiction; abnormal growth, infections, and episodes of stress. *J ournal of Pediatrics*, **83**: 1055–61.

63   Alroomi L G, Davidson J,Evans T J, *et al* (1988) Maternal narcotic abuse and the newborn. *Archives of Disease in Childhood*, 63.

64   O'Brien C P and Jaffe J H. (eds). (1990) Addictive States. *Association for research in nervous and mental disease* **70**, Raven Press, New York.

65   Kreek M J. (1983) Health Consequences associated with the use of methadone. In: Cooper J R, *et al* (eds). Research on the treatment of narcotic addiction: State of the art. *NIDA treatment research monograph series*. DHHS publication number (ADM) **83–1281**: 456–82. Rockville National Institute on Drug Abuse.

66   Bigwood C S and Coehelho A J. (1990) Methadone and caries. *British Dental Journal*, **231**.

67   Lewis D. (1990) Methadone and caries. *British Dental Journal*, **231**.

68   Dollery C Sir. (1991) *Therapeutic drugs. Methadone Hydrochloride, M92.* Churchill Livingstone, Edinburgh.

69   Reynolds J. Ed. Martindale (1993) *The Extra Pharmacopoeia*. Pharmaceutical Press, 1082.

70   Clarice ECG (ed). *Isolation and identification of drugs in pharmaceuticals,body fluids and post mortem material*. Part 2 page 408.Pharmaceutical Press, London.

71   Dollery C Sir. (1991) *Therapeutic drugs. Diamorphine Hydrochloride, D74.* Churchill Livingstone, Edinburgh.

72   *Personal Communication*. The National Poisons Unit, New Cross Hospital, London, 1994.

73   Aronow R, Brenner S L and Woolley P V. (1973) An apparent epidemic: Methadone poisioning in children. *Clinical Toxicology*, **6(2)**: 175.

74   Laurence D R and Bennett P N. (1991) Poisoning, Drug Overdose, Antidotes. *Clinical Pharmacology*, **9**: 138.

75   Stockley IH (1994) *Drug interactions: a source book of adverse interactions, their mechanisms, clinical importance and management* 3rd ed, Blackwell Scientific Publications, Oxford

76   British Medical Association and the Royal Pharmaceutical Society (1995) Appendix 1: Interactions. *British National Formulary,* **29** March.

77   Moore R A *et al*. (1987) Opiate metabolism and excretion. *Bailliers Clinical Anaethesiology.* **1**: 829–58.

78   Novick D M, *et al*. (1981) Methadone disposition in patients with chronic liver disease. *Clin Pharmacol Ther*. **30**: 353–62.

79   GMC. (1993) *Professional conduct and discipline: Fitness to practice.* **2**: 17.

80   *Medicines, ethics and practice: a guide for pharmacists.* (1995) Pharmaceutical Press.

81   Raistrick D, Bradshaw J, Tober G, *et al*. (1994) Leeds Dependence Questionnaire. *Addiction*. **89**: 563–72.

82   Ghodse H. (1995) *Drugs and Addictive Behaviour. A Guide To Treatment*. 2nd Edition, Blackwell Science Ltd. Oxford.

83   Edwards G, Arif A and Hodgeson R. (1981) Nomenculture and classification of drug and alcohol-related problems: A WHO memorandum. *Bulletin of the World Health Organisation*. **59**(2): 225–42.

84   Psychoactive Substance Abuse. *Diagnostic and Statistical Manual of the American Psychiatric Association*, 4th Edition. (1994).

85 Prochaska J O, DiClemente C and Norcross J. (1992) In search of how people change: applications to addictive behaviours. *American Psychologist.* **47**: 1102–14.

86 Bradley B, Philips G, Green L and Gossop M. (1989) Circumstances surrounding the initial lapse to opiate use following detoxification. *British Journal of Psychiatry* 1989, **154**: 354–9.

87 Cushman P and Dole V P. Detoxification of rehabilitated methadone maintained patients. *Journal of the American Medical Association*, **226**: 747,752.

88 Stimmel B, Goldberg J, Rotkopf E and Cohen M. Ability to remain abstinent after methadone detoxification: a six year study. *Journal of the American Medical Association*, **237**: 1216–20.

89 Senay E C, Dorus W, Goldberg F and Thornton W. Withdrawal from methadone maintenance: rate of withdrawal and expectation. *Archives of General Psychiatry*, **34**: 361–7.

90 Hall S M. (1979) The abstinence phobia. In: NA Krasnegor (ed). *Behavioural Analysis of Substance Abuse*, NADI Research Monograph **25**. US National Institute on Drug Abuse.

91 Ward J, Mattick R and Hall, W. (1992) *Key Issues in Methadone Maintenance Treatment.* New South Wales University Press, Australia.

92 Fleming P, Davies A, Dickson A, *et al* (1994) *Working with pregnant women who misuse drugs.* Wessex Drugs Forum.

93 Dubble, Dunne, Aldridge T and Kearney P. Registering Concern, *Community Care*, 12/3/87.

94 Reiger D A, Farmer M E, Rae D S, *et al.* (1990) Comorbidity of mental disorders with alcohol and other drug abuse: Results from the Epidemiologic Catchment Area (ECA) study. *Journal of the American Medical Association*, **264**: 2511–8.

95 Strang J. (1988) Editorial: Changing injecting practices: Blunting the habit. *British Journal of Addiction* **83**: (3).

96 Weber R, Ledergerber B, Poravil M, *et al*. (1990) Progression of HIV infection in misusers of injected drugs who stop injecting or follow a programme of maintenance treatment with methadone, *British Medical Journal*, **301**: 1362–5.

index

abscesses, 85
abstinence, 92
    abstinence phobia, 122
Addicts Index, 13, 70
adolescents, 144–5
Advisory Council on the Misuse of Drugs
(ACMD), 15, 21
AIDS and drug abuse, 15–16, 21
    methadone treatment and, 145–6
alcohol, 28, 60
    alcohol dependence, 138
    alcohol/methadone interactions, 43, 57, 60,
    83
    assessing alcohol use, 83
    poly drug use, 118, 138
amenorrhoea, 46
America see USA
Amidon, 9
amitriptyline, 61
ammonium chloride, 61
amphetamines, 118, 135
analgesia, 63
    masking underlying illness, 63, 85
    non-opiate analgesics, 63
    pain relief mechanisms, 42
Antabuse (disulfiram), 61, 138
anti-convulsants, 44, 62
    carbamazepine, 60
    phenytoin, 61
antidepressants, 61
anxiety
    about detoxification, 122
    during methadone treatment, 47
aspirin, 63
assessment, 76–88
    checklist example, 79–81
    drug-using history, 82–4, 106–7
    urinalysis, 87, 132–3
asthma, 62

barbiturates, 60
belladonna sleep treatment, 26
benzodiazepines, 28–9, 60, 137–8
    clearance times, 135
    drug-using history, 82, 118
black market see illicit sales
Bockmühl, Max, 9, 10, 11
Brain Reports, 13, 20, 21
breast-feeding, 144
BritLofex (lofexidine), 122–4
bromide sleep treatment, 26
buprenorphine, 9, 57, 60
    methadone equivalence, 109

cannabis, 71, 135, 138, 146
carbamazepine, 60
chemistry of methadone, 40
Chemists Inspecting Officers, 72
Chen, K K, 11
chest infections, 44, 85
children
    child care issues, 86, 145
    child protection, 144–5
    Children Act (1989), 144
    methadone overdose, 57, 58
    see also newborn
chloral hydrate, 60
chlormethiazole, 60
chlorpromazine, 143
cigarette smoking, 44
cimetidine, 60
cisapride, 60
clinics see drug clinics
clonidine, 122
cocaine
    clearance times, 135
    legal controls, 8, 66, 69
    prevalence in USA, 24
codeine, 60, 109

Committee on Drug Addiction, 13
Community Drug Teams (CDT), 18, 98
computerised prescriptions, 19
confidentiality, 130
    Addicts Index and, 70
    Chemists Inspecting Officers and, 72
    child protection and, 144
    during assessment, 77–8
    methadone and driving, 71
congenital abnormalities, 47, 142
constipation, 44–5, 56, 85
contract (prescribing), 131
controlled drugs, 66
    list of, 69
    methadone dispensing, 68–9
controlled trials, 24, 25
    Hartnoll et al study (1980), 14, 24
convulsions, 44
counselling, 29, 30, 90
    Nyswander & Dole study, 17, 29
crime and drug use, 82, 85, 86
    prison, 118
customs controls, 72
cyclizine, 60

Dally, Anne, 16
Dangerous Drugs Act, 8, 20
databases, 70
    Addicts Index, 13, 70
death from overdose, 44, 57, 62
Defence of the Realm Regulation (1916), 8, 20
dental decay, 50, 85
depression, 147
depression of respiration, 44, 57
desipramine, 60
detoxification, 94–5, 116–27
    abstinence not achieved, 147
    benzodiazepine detox, 137–8
    Detox Handbook, 116
    detox regimes, 120–1
    detox regimes (pros/cons), 94–5
    during pregnancy, 143
    research studies, 26–7
    treatment aims, 106
    WHO terminology, 93
    withdrawal symptoms, 59
dextromoramide, 109
dextropropoxyphene, 61
diabetes, 62
diamorphine see heroin
diazepam

clearance times, 135
    for treating convulsions, 44, 59
Diconal (dipipanone), 66, 69
    methadone equivalence, 109
dihydrocodeine, 109, 125
discovery of methadone, 9–11, 20
disulfiram, 61, 138
doctors see GPs; health professionals
Dolantin (pethidine), 9
Dole, Vincent, 17, 20, 28, 29
Dolophine (methadone), 9
domperidone, 60
driving, 70–1
    drug interactions and, 43
drowsiness/sedation, 42–3
Drug Advisory Services, 18
    ethnic communities and, 146
    inappropriate referrals, 147
drug clinics, 18–19, 98
    historical aspects, 13, 14–15, 21
drug interactions, 43, 57, 60–1
    advice on, 57
    alcohol/methadone, 43, 57, 60, 83
drug-using history, 82–4
    poly drug users, 118
Drugs, Pregnancy and Childcare, 142
dryness of mouth/eyes/nose, 44
DTF formulations, 32–3
    pros and cons, 34

economic factors, 24, 86
    cost of heroin, 110
ecstasy (MDMA), 135
Edinburgh experience, 15–16
Ehrhart, Gustav, 9, 10, 11
Eisleb, Otto, 9
Eli-Lilly pharmaceutical company, 9
employment issues, 24
epilepsy, 62
ethnic aspects, 146
euphoric effects, 41–2
    heroin v methadone, 107
export licence, 72

family situation, 86
First Brain Report (1961), 13
First Opium Convention (Hague, 1912), 8
formulations, 32–7
    injectable methadone, 34, 100–1, 139
    tablets, 33, 36, 43
Fortral (pentazocine), 109

Gee's linctus, 109
Glasgow Drug Clinic, 15
GPs (General Practitioners), 18, 98
   ethical dilemmas, 71
   Home Office notifications, 69–70
   see also maintenance prescribing

hair analysis, 134, 135
half-lives of drugs, 51–3
hallucinations, 46
Harrison Act (USA, 1914), 16, 20
Hartnoll, Richard, 14
health problems
   chest infections, 44, 85
   constipation, 44–5, 56, 85
   dental decay, 50, 85
   history taking, 85
   HIV/AIDS, 15–16, 85, 145–6
   liver disease, 62, 85
health professionals
   assessing drug users, 76–88
   attitudes towards drug users, 116–17, 136, 147
   drug addiction in, 9
   supervision and support, 138
   UK prescribing services, 18
   US experience, 16
   see also GPs
hepatitis infection, 62
heroin (diamorphine)
   assessing current use, 82–4, 118
   clearance times, 135
   dental decay and, 50
   euphoric effects, 41, 107
   half-life, 51
   heroin + methadone users, 146
   historical aspects, 9, 14–15, 20–1
   legal controls, 66, 69
   methadone equivalence, 109–10
   ounces/grams conversion, 111
   prescribing pros/cons, 102–3
   variations in purity, 106
   versus methadone in detox, 125
   versus methadone effects, 107
   withdrawal in newborn, 47
histamine release, 45–6
   asthma and, 62
historical aspects, 8–22
history taking, 76–88
   drug use, 82–4, 106–7

HIV and drug abuse, 15–16, 85
   methadone treatment and, 145–6
Hoechst A G, 11
holidays, 72, 130
Home Office
   Addicts Index, 13, 70
   address, 67, 70, 72
   Drugs Inspectorate, 71–2
   private practice guidelines, 99
hospitals
   in-patient assessments, 76
   legal controls on methadone, 69
hydrocodone, 69
hydromorphone, 69

I G Farbenindustrie, 9–11
ibuprofen, 63
illicit sales
   methadone, 19, 107–8
   Physeptone, 14
   private practice and, 19
   see also heroin
injecting drugs
   assessment of practices, 84, 87
   dependence on practice, 148
   injectable methadone, 34, 100–1, 139
Inspectorate (Home Office), 71–2
insulin sleep treatment, 26

J Collis Brown, 109
'Jacks' (heroin tablets), 14

Kleiderer report (1945), 11
Kreek, M J, 50

leakage see illicit sales
Leeds Dependence Questionnaire, 78
legal aspects, 66–73
   Children Act (1989), 144
   clients going to prison, 118
   crime and drug use, 82, 85, 86
   Medicines Act (1968), 32, 66
   methadone manufacture, 32
   Misuse of Drugs Act (1971), 66
   origin of legal controls, 8
levorphanol, 69
linctus formulations, 33, 35
liver disease, 62, 85
lofexidine, 122–4
long-term effects, 50
LSD, 135

maintenance prescribing, 96–7
  of diamorphine (heroin), 102–3
  handwriting exemptions, 67
  historical aspects, 13–17
  injectable methadone, 100–1, 139
  irresponsible prescribing, 71
  is it appropriate?, 93
  legal aspects, 66–7, 71
  long-term effects, 50
  practical issues, 130–40
  prescribing contract, 131
  prescription example, 160
  research basis, 27–9
  starting dose determinations, 104-13
  treatment choices, 96–7
  treatment termination, 121, 136–7
  UK services, 18–19, 98–9
  US experience, 16–18
manufacture regulations, 32
MAOI antidepressants, 61
Maudsley Community Drug Team, 27
MDMA (ecstasy), 135
medical conditions, 62–3
  convulsions, 44
  see also health problems
medical practitioners see health professionals
Medicines Act (1968), 32, 66
menstrual cycle disorders, 46
mental health
  history taking, 85
  problems, 147
metabolism of methadone, 51–5, 134, 135
metoclopramide, 60
miosis (small pupils), 45
Misuse of Drugs Act (1971), 66
Misuse of Drugs Tribunal, 71
Mitcheson, Martin, 14
MMT see maintenance prescribing
moclobemide, 61
morphine
  addiction statistics, 9, 14
  controlled drug, 69
  methadone equivalence, 109
motivational interviewing, 90

naloxone, 61
  for overdose reversal, 58
  for treating convulsions, 44
naltrexone, 61, 126
Narcotics Anonymous, 126

National Institute of Drug Abuse (NIDA), 28
nausea and vomiting, 43–4, 45
newborn, 47–9
  withdrawal symptoms, 13, 47–9, 143–4
  see also pregnancy
notification to Home Office, 69–70
NSAIDs, 63
Nyswander, Marie, 17, 20, 28, 29

opiates
  assessing current use, 82–4
  dihydrocodeine, 109, 125
  First Opium Convention (Hague, 1912), 8
  legal controls, 69
  methadone equivalences, 109
  opiate receptors, 41, 42, 56
  physiological effects, 40–50
  tolerance to, 56–7
  see also heroin
oral methadone, 32–3
  pros and cons, 34–5
orgasm, delayed, 46
overdose, 57–9
  accidental, 107
  causes of death, 44, 57, 62
  liver disease and, 62
  risks of, 56
  treatment of, 58–9
oxycodone, 69

pain, 63
  pain relief mechanisms, 42
palfium, 69
paracetamol, 63
parents (drug-using), 86, 145
  see also pregnancy
pentazocine, 109
periods, absence of, 46
pethidine
  discovery of, 9
  legal controls, 69
  methadone equivalence, 109
pharmacists, 32, 33, 66
  methadone destruction, 69
  methadone dispensing, 68–9
  pharmacy inspecting officers, 72
pharmacological effects, 40–50
  pharmacokinetics, 51–5, 134, 135
  tolerance, 56–7
phenazocine, 69

phenobarbitone, 61
phenytoin, 61
Physeptone, 12, 13
    on illicit market, 14
    Physeptone Linctus, 33
    tablets, 33, 36
physiological effects, 40–9
    long-term, 50
piritamide, 69
polamidon, 9, 11
police, 70, 72
poly drug users, 118
possession of methadone, 66
pregnancy and methadone, 142–4
    amenorrhoea and, 46
    cord blood levels, 51
    effects on newborn, 13, 47–9, 143–4
prescribing/prescriptions
    coping with requests, 77
    irresponsible prescribing, 71
    legal aspects, 66–7, 71
    preparations available, 32–7
    prescription example, 160
    reasons for requests, 93
    UK services, 18–19
    see also maintenance prescribing
prison, 118
private medical practice, 18, 19, 98–9
psychiatric problems, 85
psychosocial interventions, 29, 30
    Nyswander & Dole study, 17, 29
pupil constriction, 45, 56

receptors (opiate), 41, 42, 56
recreational drug use, 138
registered addicts, 70
Rehab Handbook, 116
relapses, 91–2, 126, 147
research aspects, 24–30
    research methods, 24–6
    urinalysis and, 133
respiratory depression, 44, 57
rifampicin, 61
Rolleston report (1926), 8–9, 20

Schaumann, O, 9
Second Brain Report (1965), 13
sedation/drowsiness, 42–3
selegiline, 61
Severity of Opiate Dependence
Questionnaire, 78

sexual desire alterations, 46
Sheffield experience, 16
side-effects of methadone, 41–9
    tolerance to, 56
SIDS (Sudden Infant Death Syndrome), 49
sleep treatment, 26
sleep-promoting effects, 43
smoking
    cigarettes, 44
    heroin, 62
sodium bicarbonate, 61
sodium thiocyanate, 26
SODQ (Severity of Opiate Dependence
Questionnaire), 78
spillage see illicit sales
street agencies, 18
Substance Abuse Assessment Questionnaire,
78
Sudden Infant Death Syndrome, 49
suppositories, 34
sweating, 46

tablet formulations, 33, 36
    'Jacks' (heroin), 14
    reasons for requests for, 36, 43
Temgesic (buprenorphine), 9, 57, 60
    methadone equivalence, 109
tolerance, 56–7
tooth decay, 50
travel, 72, 130
treatment, 90–104, 116–27
    harm reduction, 92
    motivation and change, 90–2
    terminating, 121, 136–7
    see also detoxification; maintenance
    prescribing
tricyclic antidepressants, 61

UK Pharmacy Act (1869), 20
unemployment issues, 24
urinalysis, 132–5
    at assessment, 87, 132–3
urinary urgency/difficulty, 45
urine acidifiers, 61
urine alkalinisers, 61
USA
    drugs policy, 16–18, 20–1, 24
    research studies, 24–6, 28–9

vomiting/nausea, 43–4

weight gain, 47
  withdrawal symptoms and, 59
weight loss, 85
withdrawal symptoms, 59
  abstinence phobia, 122
  from benzodiazepines, 137
  methadone *v* heroin, 125
  naloxone-induced, 58
  in newborn babies, 13, 47–8, 143–4
  pregnancy and, 143
  pseudo-withdrawal syndrome, 122
  research studies, 26–7
workers *see* health professionals

young people, 144-5

zidovudine, 61
zopiclone, 61

Appendix

Dose ready reckoner

7 and 14 x all commonly prescribed doses

Daily dose	7 days total dose	14 days total dose
2.5mg	17.5mg	35mg
3mg	21mg	42mg
5mg	35mg	70mg
7.5mg	52.5mg	105mg
8mg	56mg	112mg
10mg	70mg	140mg
12.5mg	87.5mg	175mg
15mg	105mg	210mg
17.5mg	122.5mg	245mg
20mg	140mg	280mg
25mg	175mg	350mg
30mg	210mg	420mg
35mg	245mg	490mg
40mg	280mg	560mg
45mg	315mg	630mg
50mg	350mg	700mg
55mg	385mg	770mg
60mg	420mg	840mg
65mg	455mg	910mg
70mg	490mg	980mg
75mg	525mg	1050mg
80mg	560mg	1120mg
85mg	595mg	1190mg
90mg	630mg	1260mg
95mg	665mg	1330mg
100mg	700mg	1400mg

Prescribing aide memoire

Methadone is a controlled drug. If it is not correctly prescribed, on the correct pad, the pharmacist may be unable to dispense. For full details see Section 5: Methadone and the law.

Example:
Methadone mixture 1mg/1mL (one mg/one mL)
30mg (thirty milligrams) daily for 14 days
Total 420mg (four hundred and twenty milligrams)
Dispense daily (two days Saturday)